How To Draw Your Boundaries

and why no one else can save you

This book is dedicated to my friend Dan.
I didn't know you, but you were there.

Of course I'll hurt you.
Of course you'll hurt me.
Of course we will hurt each other.
But this is the very condition of existence.
To become spring means accepting the
risk of winter.
To become presence means accepting the
risk of absence.

— Antoine de Saint-Exupery

Author's Note:

Any reference to time across the book "a month ago, a week ago", respects when the essay was written.

Contents

Introduction

This pandemic and the need to socially distance tested all my boundary setting skills. It reminded me that when it comes to setting boundaries, we are all amateurs.

I took notes of things I recently learned and collected pieces I've written in the past in an attempt to assemble a manual focused on boundaries: where to start, what they are for, how to express them, how to enforce them and what they sound like.

This means this collection does include essays you might also come across in my other books.

I hope reading through this is as helpful to you as creating it was for me.

DZ

Self-Love

How It Begins

I think it all begins when I feel completely lost. When I feel stuck, like the same things keep happening to me over and over.

I've tried everything, and still cannot seem to get the approval or love that I look for in others. I feel misunderstood and isolated.

I decide I've had enough.

I may not find what I need in others, but, I have me.

I need to learn how to stand by me — how to be the one who believes in me and supports me.

This means learning to make peace with the fact others might be disappointed or confused by my decisions.

I start to believe in my own self-worth, as something I inherently have rather than something I need to earn. My self-worth is related just to being, not with doing or achieving.

I begin working towards giving more breath and life to what I think and what I want. This means I become more disciplined, more deliberate, more directed. Very slowly I see the results of the actions I take.

As I begin to see results, I see that I cannot impact other people's opinions of me. I have to remain focused on feeding my own opinion of me. This is how getting others to like me begins to become less important — in part because it would require that I distract myself from my own endeavors, and in part because I've learned I can't have an impact over what others feel or do.

I begin to care for myself, talk to myself and do things for myself that normally were reserved for others. I take me to the doctor, stop berating myself, become aware of my critical inner voice and begin to shift it towards being more loving and compassionate towards me.

I become increasingly comfortable with saying no — in particular to make room for all the things I want to do to honor myself.

My relationships begin to change. I lose people who seem unable to adjust to the fact that I am doing right by me.

I feel my life is tight, so tight. I need space to reconsider everything. I need to spend more time alone. I feel like nothing is what it seems.

I begin questioning my own belief system. If my thoughts tell me I'm not enough, could it be my thoughts are lying to me? I begin to see how my feelings and my thoughts change the way I perceive things and are not necessarily true.

This interesting, sometimes painful, ultimately very beautiful trajectory is what it feels like to begin to learn to love myself.

How Do I Become Emotionally Independent?

In the quest for happiness and emotional independence, the single most important thing you can do is learn to love yourself.

How you feel about yourself is a lens that has an impact over how you perceive everything.

Loving yourself is the dedicated practice of two steps: setting boundaries and spending time alone.

Boundaries are about being clear with where your limits are, and time alone turns the volume down on the world so you can hear yourself. This is how you get to know what you want, what you need, and how you make space to express yourself through creating something.

Emotional independence does not mean you don't need anyone else. It means you create interdependent, rather than codependent relationships.

The difference is that in a codependent relationship, you expect the other person to do what you should be doing for yourself.

In an interdependent relationship, you support each other. You witness each other's emotional evolution. You share your lives without panic, without despair, without neediness, without clinging. You never put each other down.

5

Emotional independence is never about needing no one. It's about the knowledge that true, healthy connection is the meaning of life.

Truth Bullet

When I understood what I am about to tell you I felt I had been shot with a truth bullet.

Here is is: The best things in life happen without my intervention.

I don't have to convince, persuade or chase anyone or win anyone over to get or catch either a good friend or a significant other.

Love — in any iteration — is like gravity. I don't do anything to keep my feet firmly planted on the ground.

These things are so true that if I instead decide to act — to exert effort, to work at it, to aggressively pursue, to supervise everything — I attract unhealthy relationships and wonder where to cast the blame.

I walk away from any dynamic that requires me to compromise my peace of mind. I do less. A lot less. I do nothing and witness an upside down life right itself.

Love Yourself

Loving yourself is not something you do but something you practice, a series of interconnected actions that involve treating yourself like something special and wonderful.

You eat well and exercise and do things to gently assist you in the battles that you fight — for example, I have anxiety and do my best to go to yoga, breathe, get a good night of sleep. I work hard at defying my own thoughts.

No Dushka. What you worry about is not going to happen.

You step away from things that hurt you — friends who put you down or the job that doesn't fulfill or inspire you or the guy who, well, doesn't do what he says he's going to do.

You can do better, not because you can go find another man but because you have yourself.

You do things for you that you would do for someone you love — fun things like getting you those shoes you like and harder things like standing up for yourself, or following through on your own promises.

This is important because every time you do you teach yourself you are worth trusting.

I can't go get drinks. I said I'd go to the gym four times a week and I skipped yesterday.

You do things that make you happy and let you get to know yourself and get really involved in creating something. A pie, a garden, a book. It doesn't matter what. It's yours and it's for you and maybe also supports others.

You take ownership of everything that affects your vital space — you build sacred things like habits and ceremony and boundaries. You come to terms with disappointing others. You learn to say no.

You say yes a lot too and surprise yourself by making unexpected plans — yes, yes. Book the trip to go see the Northern Lights. Get that beautiful painting so you can place it over your bed. Drink every day out of a beautiful hand made cup.

Do senseless things, less for the objective and more for the sheer pleasure of it.

People who love themselves don't always. Loving yourself is like every other feeling — inconsistent, fluid, sometimes dismaying — but in the end you build a relationship with someone truly interesting you know you can count on.

Social Media

Sometimes on social media I get a message that is cruel, aggressive or combative.

I click on that person's profile and see, ten times out of ten, that the person is cruel, aggressive or combative with everyone, not just with me.

This is how I've learned that how a person reacts to me has nothing to do with me.

I spend a lot of time on social media and have learned to exercise the power that I have over the spaces I frequent. I want to be nourished, not depleted.

By nourished I mean I want love, respect, intelligence — I don't need to be agreed with, but I do need to not be baited or provoked.

This lesson — I decide what I allow in my periphery — has served me well both online and off.

Social media has taught me how to set boundaries. I can see that you want to argue. If I am to be a part of this argument, I get to decide if I want to engage in it, and I don't.

The reason is simple: I'd rather spend time writing than spend that same time making a point to a stranger on the internet.

Convincing you to see things my way is not interesting to me. I offer my perspective. If it's useful to you, that's great. If it's not, that's great too.

This is how social media has taught me to be careful with how I use my time and my energy.

Many people on social media ask me for direct advice. I never give it. I write about what I've learned from my experiences and hope others find them helpful, but that's different from providing direct advice to someone I have no context for.

Social media has taught me to encourage people to listen to the most valuable voice they will ever hear: their own.

Through the years, regular interactions on social media have given me a solid handle on the elements that tend to make something I write go viral. Every day I make a choice: do I write about what I want to say, or do I cater to your clicks?

I have things to say, and to me that trumps how you react to them.

Social media reminds me every day to listen to myself rather than seek another person's reaction to my words.

I don't know what others learn from social media. But I've also determined that the only experience I can speak from is my own.

Who Do You Love So Much You'd Take Back No Matter What?

This question hides within it a lethal blind spot.

Can you see it?

This question assumes that taking someone back "no matter what" is related to my amount of love to them.

Taking someone back after they have done something terrible is not an effect of massive love.

It's an effect of low self-esteem and poor boundaries.

I can't control what I feel towards another.

If they hurt me, I will leave, and my departure will have nothing to do with the depth or size or sincerity or earnestness of my love.

I'll leave because I love myself, because I deserve more than "no matter what". And, so do you, my friend. So do you.

Noise

Figuring out what is the best way to be living your life is like trying to listen to soft music in a room with deafening noise.

You need to stop listening to all the noise and start listening to your own soft music.

The noise comes from people who feel they know what is best for you. Mostly they are very well intentioned, but here is the thing. They are not you. They are your parents, your family members, your friends, your boss, even your own brain (once it internalizes all the noise).

Noise sounds like this:
Why is everyone doing better than me?
Will that choice make you money?
Should you really be doing that?
Sure, it looks fun but you could get hurt.
Be careful.
You are not doing it right!
You are not good enough.
What will other people say?
Do you really think you can make a career out of that?
But that's not what's best — what my parents would want — the reasonable option!

The way to listen to your soft music is to pay attention to how things make you feel; that thing you like makes you elated or excited or giddy or you feel dread.

Or pay attention when the soft music uses your body to try to tell you what not to do:
The appointment you are always late for.
The document you just can't write.
The recurring headache.
Insomnia.
Restlessness.
Anxiety.

In my opinion, listening to that soft music and not listening to everything else will show you the way.

The more you fine-tune your listening, the easier it becomes.

Get Away

Get away from anyone who is cruel to you, who wants to diminish you, who puts you down, who tries to control you, who hurts you or who frightens you.

But Dushka! What if they are family?

Get away from anyone who is cruel to you, who wants to diminish you, who puts you down, who tries to control you, who hurts you or who frightens you.

It doesn't matter who they are.

The Boss

One of the biggest mind-shifts I've ever had to do was fully own the fact that I am the one who decides.

I see this at work a lot: what keeps an employee from becoming a manager is the ability to shift from asking a lot of questions to answering them. From *"what should I do?"* to *"here is what you need to do".*

This agency is the main ingredient in becoming an adult. It's not that you suddenly know more — we are all winging it — it's that you come into the fact you have both power and free will.

We like asking for permission because it releases us from responsibility. *"Tell me what to do"* is less scary than deciding.

What should I do with my life? What should I study in college? Should I break up with him? Should I be angry? Do I stay or go?

Often we ask for advice because we are hesitant to be fully responsible for the consequences.

The price to pay is that you are giving your life away to others. Your life is in effect the sum of the decisions that you make. Your decisions, however small, are too precious to relinquish to others.

Your life belongs to you. Become the sole owner of it.

Self-Acceptance

Finding happiness is an adventure. And because everything changes and you change you have to start this adventure over and over again.

A good way to start on this complex, wonderful process is to take a good look at what you are and accept it. From this place of loving acceptance you can find people like you who define happiness in the same way.

You stop asking questions like: *Am I normal? Is there something wrong with me? Should I try to be something other than what I am?* (The answers are: yes, no and please no.)

The worst way to start on this complex, wonderful process is to force yourself to be something you are not. You will be met with the strongest, most primal, most desperate resistance. You will end up surrounded by the wrong people (for you). You will condemn yourself to perpetual inadequacy.

You will wake up one morning wondering how on earth you ended up in the wrong life.

Improving yourself — striving to be a better person — is essential to happiness.

Changing yourself — trying to be something you aren't will make you angry, bitter, resentful, hopeless, lonely.

Believe me when I tell you who you already are is perfect. Go find that. Accept that. Love that. Amplify it. Be proud of it. Hold it up so others like you can find you.

How Do You Stop Pleasing People?

Life is hard. Really hard. Finding my way takes grit and mostly means two things:

Making a distinction between what works for "everyone" and what works for me.

Finding the presence of mind to disappoint others in the name of standing up for myself.

People-pleasing is disguised as generosity but really it's avoidance. It's constant, relentless escape from doing the hard work of not compromising myself.

The price is to not clearly understand who I am, to let people walk all over me, to feel full of bitterness and resentment and to wonder why I feel I am in the wrong life.

I am in the wrong life because if I people-please I don't understand how to set boundaries and constantly allow others to make decisions for me.

Love yourself. Love yourself enough to know you are worth not betraying yourself in the name of getting others to approve of you.

What Behaviors Indicate That I Love Myself?

I treat myself like I would treat a loving friend, with compassion, patience, consideration. No berating. No trash talking.

I treat others the same way — no gossip, judging, putting others down.

I have clear boundaries and know how to set them, move them and stand by them.

I am aware of how my insecurities warp my perceptions, so I am able to regard things with a bit more clarity.

I know who I am and am not afraid to express it.

I like being alone.

I am almost always creating something.

I take care of myself and it feels valuable and necessary rather than selfish.

I stay away from things that hurt me.

I keep the promises I make to myself.

I feel proud of my efforts even if they are invisible to others.

I recognize that I am and always will be a work in progress.

What Should I Do in My 20s to Avoid Regrets?

As quickly as you can, learn to make your own decisions. This means making peace with the fact you will often disappoint others.

As quickly as you can, accept you cannot manage what others think of you. This means making peace with the fact that sometimes you will not be liked, that time and time again you will be misunderstood, and that you are not for everyone.

Tell people how you feel. If you say *"I love you"* and the person does not love you back you might feel temporary discomfort but in the grand scheme of things stating where you stand with your mind and with your heart is splendid.

Make it a habit to tell the truth as often and as clearly as possible. This does not run counter to being kind, but it does run counter to white lies.

Take notice of the people who love you. Are you treating them well? Are you taking them for granted?

Anything you do right now will accumulate over time, so get busy creating habits that line up with what you want for later. If in your 20s you write a single page a day, you will have (at least) a book to publish in your 30s. This applies to anything at all.

Embrace experiences. Say yes if you are curious. An example of very bad advice is *"you only regret what you don't do"* and that's blatantly untrue — so take care of yourself. But also know that what you experience makes for a rich life, and in a very real way experiences are the only way you ever learn anything.

Learn about self-compassion. Don't treat yourself the way you would never treat another. I cannot stress enough how important this is: you don't want your worst enemy to be the person who is with you every second of every day.

Learn to love yourself. If you don't know how, figure it out. Your feelings about yourself — your inner dialogue, your sense of confidence, your insecurities — will shape everything.

Illusion

Comparing yourself to others is so painful, and so useless: it's an illusion. You can't possibly know what is truly going on in someone else's life.

You are looking out when you should be looking in.

In other words, you are spending time and energy on your own delusions. They might or might not be real.

Please don't fall into the trap of assuming that things would improve if only you got a job — a promotion — material success.

There is nothing outside of you that will make this better. This requires an internal adjustment.

You need to exercise turning all the focus on yourself, what you want to accomplish and how you want to live your life.

The clearer you are on the nature of your own path, the less you will worry about what others are doing and the more you will realize that you cannot possibly desire, covet or miss out on what doesn't truly interest you.

You will understand and respect that things unfold differently for every one of us.

The busier you are working on you, your life and your happiness, the less time you will have to dwell on another's success other than to celebrate it.

OMG, Stop It With the Excuses

It's incredible to me, the things we justify and make excuses for in the name of keeping something we are afraid to lose.

"He does lie to me about important things but really not very often."

"Sometimes she is mean to me but she loves me."

"He can be abusive but he works a lot and is under a lot of pressure."

"It's true he can't take care of himself but since I met him he's made so much progress."

Pay attention to what you refuse to see.

In the end the decisions that you make determine who stays in your life and how people treat you once they are in it.

How Can I Be Myself?

In my experience, this is less about being and more about exploring.

By this I mean it's a process, takes a long time, and has an evolution (meaning, it changes. You change.).

I ask myself what I want and then am curious about what happens when I get it. (*Hmmm. I thought that was what I wanted but I guess not.*)

I look for the things that I like and that are important to me.

I identify the things that are not me and do less of them. (*I understand cars are sexy but honestly. I could not possibly care any less what you drive.*)

Sometimes this is hard because a lot of other people like certain things, so not liking them makes me feel like there is something wrong with me (Nope. I'm OK.).

A few examples I can think of:

Being at a party and arriving home late and wondering why I feel so exhausted and so hollowed out. (I don't like parties.)

Being alone for many days at a time and wondering why I feel so empty. (I love social interaction — I just need time to recharge.)

Writing and feeling electric, plugged into the whole universe. (Yep. This is it. This is what I want more, more, more of.)

Falling in love and getting married and feeling like that ring felt like a noose. Marriage is wonderful. Just because something is wonderful doesn't mean it's right for me.

So that's what you do — step. Review. Step. How do I feel? Step. What do I need? Step. Why does this feel awful when it's supposed to feel wonderful?

This exploration is not tiresome or stressful (well, OK. Sometimes it is.). But mostly it's the delightful discovery of this interesting person that you are. You get to know her, and slowly, astonishingly, you become yourself.

What Might I Be Missing Out On?

The older I get the more I realize I don't know what I want. Keeping my options open, rather than feeling like I have to decide, determine, label or choose, has considerably improved my life.

That being said, I'm very clear on what I *don't* want. Even if what I don't want might create internal tension.

Here is an example:

I go out of my way to avoid parties and noisy places. I love my friends but most frequently want to be home (or with small groups of people).

Then I find out someone threw a party and didn't invite me and feel left out.

I let myself feel whatever I'm feeling but, hey. I don't like parties. If the price of not having to go to one is feeling a teeny bit excluded I sit peacefully with that.

The feeling soon dissipates.

You learn to be more comfortable with the notion you are missing out when you know you are exactly where you want to be. You can't "miss out" on something you are not interested in doing.

If you work on finding yourself, what you are missing out on is nothing.

Self-Centered

There are many meanings to the term "self-centered". The first is independent, sovereign, self-reliant, not easily influenced by others.

The concept of loving yourself, caring for yourself, might be self-centered but is not selfish. It is designed for you to give yourself what you need so you can in turn give to others from a healthier, rather than depleting place.

Loving yourself makes giving sustainable.

Being self-centered can also refer to someone mostly interested in herself. This can lead to carelessness or intolerance. A self-centered person can be selfish: devoted to herself, to the exclusion of others instead of for others.

Breakfast

You keep hearing breakfast is the most important meal of the day, but are never hungry in the morning.

Let me share with you one of the most difficult, most useful things to understand to arrive at a better life.

Just because something works for everyone else doesn't mean it works for me.

Just because something doesn't work for anyone doesn't mean it won't work for me.

Each person needs to evaluate every single thing to, in effect, start from scratch.

To disregard what works for others in order to discover what works for me.

What works for others is just noise — an impediment to understanding myself.

What I think is important and what others think is important does not matter. What matters is what works for you.

Are you hearing breakfast is important, but you don't want to eat breakfast? Then don't have breakfast.

Apply this same process to everything.

To Protect Myself, Should I Be Dishonest and Selfish?

There is another possibility, you know. You can be honest and not allow anyone to take advantage of you.

The assumption that only dishonesty and selfishness can protect you from the transgressions of others is toxic.

Your own belief system locks you into a place where you can never create healthy relationships with others without a sense that you are jeopardizing your interests.

I offer you this instead: be forthcoming. Be generous. Work on setting healthy boundaries.

Prove yourself wrong.

It's a glorious thing, to leave behind a belief that pretty much guarantees your unhappiness.

What Should I Never Do?

Believe the voice inside you that whispers any version of *"you are not enough."* It can sound like *"you are too young"* or *"you are too old"* or *"your best work is behind you"* or *"you are not strong".*

Compromise who you are in an effort to get someone to love you.

Crave validation from people who don't lead a life you'd want for yourself.

Look for happiness in events that are supposed to be milestones.

Berate yourself.

Do something that doesn't really interest you because it's what "everybody" does.

Say "I'm fine" when you are not.

Feel like you need to read someone else's mind.

Feel guilty about setting boundaries.

Apologize when you say no.

Explain or justify your choices.

Stay past the point when you'd rather go home.

Wonderful

When I was ten or eleven my friends frequently invited me for sleepovers and pajama parties.

I would tell them my parents had not given me permission to go, but the truth is I never asked.

I never asked because spending the night at someone else's house filled me with anxiety.

It wasn't until almost two decades later that I learned I was an introvert — someone who liked people and had many friends yet needed to be alone to recharge.

A sleepover left me no space to be alone if I needed to — it left me without recourse, without options. It made me feel trapped.

You know what, in retrospect, I find most surprising? Not the introversion part, but how quick I was to assume there was something terribly wrong with me.

I didn't think *"sleepovers are not my thing, and that's OK"* but rather *"oh my god — everyone is super excited about this thing that fills me with angst. What on earth is wrong with me?"*

The biggest lesson to me is to say *"I don't like this thing that everyone likes, and that's OK"* rather than *"I have to force myself to do this because the fact that I don't like it obviously means it's something I need to adjust."*

I've learned to trust myself, but mostly to accept myself for who I am.

I like what I like, I don't like what I don't like, and that is OK.

Actually, it's more than OK.

It's wonderful.

Why Don't I Fit Into the Way the World Works?

There is no "way the world works".

You live in a world of worlds, worlds that are so alike they overlap, worlds so different and distant it's a wonder you can even make out their borders at all.

All these worlds exist in the same time, the same place, the same dimension.

They are all right here.

The way to find your world, where the population is your tribe, your clan, your crowd, is to step into who you are instead of making an effort to fit in.

As you do this — as you express your personality, your preferences, your choices, clarify your demands, outline your boundaries, as you are willing to let others down to stay true to yourself, the world where you belong makes itself increasingly evident and bright.

If you lament that you don't fit in but spend a lot of time trying, if you do what you do because it's what others do and not because you think you should, if you make choices in an effort to please, then your world sits close by but just beyond your grasp, invisible, locked behind a door you cannot open, because the only key is the full expression of yourself.

Find yourself, find your world.

Recast Everything

I know I'm repeating myself, but we learn what we repeat. So I will say it again, and again, and again.

Our relationship with ourselves sets the tone for every other relationship.

I try to be the person others want me to be, instead of the person I really am.

I believe every story my ego spins. That I'm not enough, that I'm stuck, that other people have better lives than mine.

I try to look for success and fulfillment outside of myself: a better house, a better car, a good husband. I will value myself when I get promoted. I will value myself when I have children.

If I look for people who can save me, fix me or approve of me I am likely to feel stuck or like I have no control over what happens to me. I feel overwhelmed and approach my relationships with despair.

If I don't know how to set boundaries I cannot respect the boundaries of another, since I don't understand them and interpret them as a form of rejection.

If I disregard my own feelings I am likely to show little empathy for the feelings of another.

If I don't take responsibility for myself, my decisions, my actions, I blame others for my circumstances and become increasingly powerless and bitter.

If I make commitments to myself and fail me, I am likely to fail others.

Self-love — asking myself what I can give to myself, questioning my own stories, assuming full responsibility for everything I am, following through on the promises I make to myself — will recast everything.

How Can I Focus on Myself More?

First, forever abandon the notion that self-care is selfish. This belief is destructive and ensures you end up isolated, resentful and depleted. This belief is why people burn out.

Ask yourself what you need. A bath? An orange? A divorce? What you need is hard to determine but the more you find time alone and the more patient you are with yourself the clearer the answer will become.

Consider learning how to meditate. It's the most glorious gift you will ever present yourself with: permission to set it all aside to make room for your breath.

Treat yourself like you would someone you love. With compassion, with generosity, with tolerance. *It's ok, Dushka. I've got you.*

Learn to say no. Boundaries are integral to this effort and saying no is a good start.

Make choices for you. If someone else tells you you are thinking of you instead of them, if they want to push you in a way that is to your detriment and their benefit — well, think about that.

Watch what you eat. Give yourself nutritious food. Make sure you are sleeping well. Learn how to breathe. Deep breaths change your life — they tell your body you are OK. Eventually breathing deeply pulls you out of feeling like life is something you have to survive.

Move. Exercise. Find something you like — or more than one thing — so it's less of an effort and more of a respite, a vacation, a reward.

Find pleasure. I will give you a tip: it's in your senses. Things that feel good, taste good, sound good. Beauty is primal and necessary. Surround yourself with it.

The meaning of life is in connection. Identify people who inspire you and build you up and keep them near you.

Create something. A book. A garden. A dish. A company. We are creators.

There is solace and peace in repetition. Find your habits. Find your rituals. Find your ceremony. Serve yourself coffee every morning in silence. Pour it into a beautiful hand made cup. Write down things you are grateful for as you sip. Do it again, and again, and again.

Finally, these are not changes you make. This is a new life you step into. It's a practice, and you come back to it over and over. Did you say yes when you wanted to say no? It's ok. It's ok. You will try again tomorrow.

Comfort Zone/Boundaries

Breaking your boundaries feels like self-betrayal, like you have turned your back on yourself. It fills you with resentment — which is anger at yourself, disguised as anger towards another person.

Getting out of your comfort zone feels frightening but there is a sense of expansion, of breaking out of that place holding you in. You know that on the other side, instead of bitterness and displeasure, what you will feel is free.

What Is a Boundary?

Why Are Boundaries Needed in Relationships?

Boundaries are needed so you can determine where you end and the other person begins.

So you can clearly outline your own precious sovereignty and unequivocally respect that of the other person.

You establish boundaries immediately, they are essential everywhere and they always make a difference.

Does Saying No Make Me a Bad Person?

A good person is one in possession of a solid moral compass, who has the tendency to do the right thing. Other ingredients might be kindness, virtue, generosity.

A person who is unable to say no has poor boundaries and compromises herself, usually in an attempt to be liked or approved of. This typically results in resentment and bitterness and in blaming others for the lack of clarity or determination.

Are People With Good Hearts Unlucky in Love?

This is a trap disguised as a question.

It contains within it a hypothesis.

If I choose to believe it, my relationships are destined to be unhealthy.

It implies: I must be cruel to be lucky in relationships.

This is simply not true.

My guess — and it's just a guess — is that we confuse a "good heart" with someone who has not set clear boundaries.

An absence of boundaries is not "nice". It's not related to goodness or selflessness. It's related to not believing I am worth loving.

My fear: If I lay down my boundaries people might not like me.

As I learn to establish boundaries, people who knew me as a person who always said yes and who always tried to please others will react, since they are seeing someone different from who they are used to.

Oh my god you have changed so much.

They might stay or go, but my firm boundary setting will begin to attract the right kind of people. The kind of people who respect who I am and the rules I establish for interacting with me.

Good hearted people treat others with compassion, with love, with kindness. This begins by being compassionate, loving and kind to yourself.

Characteristics of a Healthy Relationship

You feel safe and at peace. The relationship feels sturdy rather than an emotional roller coaster filled with drama, turmoil, chaos and disquiet.

You assume the best of each other.

You are a team. You support and encourage each other. There is no criticism, no fixing, no belittling, no using things you say against you.

Your relationship has withstood disagreement. Actually, how you disagree tells you a lot. During disagreements you seek growth and understanding rather than mutual destruction. When you fight you take responsibility rather than resorting to blame, accusations, and using words like "never" and "always".

You feel like a whole person, rather than like half of a couple. You have interests, friends, activities that don't involve your significant other, and he does too. This makes both of you happy, rather than worried, uncomfortable, suspicious, possessive.

You carve out time alone.

The relationship leaves room for evolution. *"You've changed"* is a compliment.

You set boundaries that are respected without friction, and are respectful of the boundaries of the other.

You are responsible for how you feel, and he is responsible for how he feels. The other is your partner, your accomplice, not your flotation device. You are, in fact, an excellent swimmer.

How Do You Recognize
Your Boundaries?

Something makes me uncomfortable, drained, stressed, indignant or resentful.

Something makes me feel afraid, something makes me question myself, something makes me feel guilty or selfish.

I notice the feeling and — *wait a minute Dushka what exactly is making you feel this way? Go back. What happened? Can you pinpoint it? Can you put it into words?*

Why did that hurt? Why am I so tired? Why do I feel taken advantage of? Why do I feel like I can't say no? Why do I feel I deserve better? Why do I feel I'm giving too much?

And, so that we don't feel this way again, what are we going to do to put this feeling where it belongs?

What comes next is the boundary, and it might sound complex, like *"I feel taken advantage of and I know it's not your fault because I keep offering to help. I think I love you very much and overextend myself and it has nothing to do with you."*

Or, it might sound simple, like *"no"*.

Should I Change for You?

When someone asks something of me (boss, significant other, parent) I ask myself the following:

Would this be good for me? Help me grow? Be a better person? Would this effort improve my life across other areas?

Or

Is this request akin to me becoming someone I am not?

If the request falls in the first category, I work on it. It might be uncomfortable, but this is how we grow. This is how we look back and marvel at how far we've come.

If the request falls into the second category, my answer is no.

Have You Had to Set Boundaries in Your Relationship?

Yes, definitely. Yes, always.

A boundary is not a bad thing. It's not something you suddenly have to do. It's not an extreme measure, punishment, a last resort or something you do because you have no choice.

A boundary happens right away, is natural, and is necessary for any healthy relationship.

Clear boundaries means less assumptions, less guesswork, less misunderstandings and less transgressions. They mean less confusion.

A boundary might be *"I am easily drained by social interaction so I can't stay at a party for very long."* Or *"I had a difficult day and need a bit of space. Can I call you back in an hour? I want to give you my full attention."*

Boundaries are about what you need, what you prefer, what you like, what your priorities are, and whatever puts you in a place to bring the best of you into the relationship.

I'm Having a Baby. How Can I Tell My Family Not to Help?

When I set boundaries, these are the steps I take:

First, preparation. Setting boundaries is my right. It's not an act of aggression. It's not a form of betrayal. It's not awful. It's not selfish. It's not the reflection of a terrible person.

Boundaries are love, and they are healthy. They are an expression of self-care.

Boundaries often make me feel really awful.

Reminding myself of all this is helpful because it calms me, and how I approach this will set the tone for how it will go. If I come at it agitated, guilty, defensive, what I elicit is different than if I'm sure, calm, grounded, firm.

Second, setting the boundary itself. It should be clear, clean, as simple as possible. *"I know you wanting to come over is a show of love and support but I am feeling like this is an important, complex time for my husband and for me and what we need is space."*

Third, holding the boundary. This means I might need to outline it more than once, and enforce it with the same calm, firmness and clarity.

"This is the most important time of my life, which is why I don't want to remember it as an argument or a fight. Thank you for understanding."

Finally, I find it helps to keep the door open to recognize that many times boundaries are fluid rather than static, in particular if I myself am not certain about how things will develop. *"Right now what I feel I need is space, and time. But if I realize I need the help I won't hesitate to ask for it. Thank you so much for offering to be here with me."*

When Did You First Place Boundaries?

First, I did not exist, and then my parents created me from nothing.

It was because of their contribution to my existence, their design of my genetic code and their arrangement of my cells that they felt they had authority over my life and its trajectory.

And of course at first they did.

Dushka, drink your milk. Eat your vegetables. Go to school. Do your homework. Do your very best. Dushka, you are not this but that.

But, where is the line? Where is the line between their love and my sovereignty?

My first lesson in personal boundaries was my parents. I needed boundaries to protect who I was from their ferocious, overwhelming love.

These boundaries were not acts of rebellion but a gradual, personal, healthy declaration of independence, necessary for life to belong to the person living it.

Why Do We Need to Say No?

"No" is a boundary in its simplest form.

It means I respect myself. That I love myself. That I stand up for myself. That I am willing to not do what someone is asking me to do to make room for what I want to do.

"No" means that I gradually learn how to listen to myself instead of being worried that another person is going to love me or approve of me less if I don't do what they want me to.

I understand that's important to you, but I don't want to do it and that's important to me.

As I learn to say no, my self-worth becomes stronger. I learn how to communicate more clearly. I become less afraid of the impact this word will have on another person and on our relationship. I worry less about what others will think of me. I realize that I have someone who's got my back and who I can always, always count on: me.

Confession

I have a confession to make.

I like people-pleasing.

I like doing things with and for other people, in particular when it feels like a joyful, natural co-creation, in particular when giving something of me feels like the best use of what I have to give.

It's the best.

I just have to be careful that I don't swing from *"I feel open and generous towards you"* to *"I feel resentful because I have come to see it's not how you feel towards me."*

I don't want to feel like what I do is being taken for granted or like I'm being taken advantage of.

Every relationship I have is built on certain principles. I get to know someone and natural dynamics are established. If I have always people-pleased and I decide I want to stop it with the people-pleasing, if I want to stand by me instead of feeling resentful, I am in essence altering — betraying — the tacit rules of our original arrangement.

I used to say yes to everything and now I am putting me first. It stands to reason that this will shift every single one of my relationships.

The people who react to this first are, obviously, the people I've been bending myself for the most: this is where my change is most noticeable. They don't like it, because they have grown comfortable with getting everything from me. *No, Dushka. What has gotten into you? Let's go back to the way things were.*

If these people value me they will come to realize that a new balance has been in order for some time and that my new rules are only fair.

If they instead value how convenient I made everything, how comfortable they are benefiting from me overextending myself, the relationship might not recover.

At first, this hurts like a fire in my heart.

But then, then, as the pain begins to recede, look at all the space I've made. Look at the room I have, the energy I can put into relationships that are better for me.

I am recovering, and now I feel free.

See, I made it so easy for you to use me, and now my life is better without you in it.

So, yes. Discovering who you are, shifting into being fully you, is a tough, painful road. But let me tell you. It's the best thing you will ever do.

Why Does a Close Relationship Need Boundaries?

Discovering and clearly outlining your boundaries is how you love yourself: a boundary means you put your own needs over another person's demands on you.

Learning how to state your boundaries is really necessary, really difficult and an act of courage. It implies you have to love yourself and respect your needs enough to say *"I am willing to disappoint you. If you think less of me or lose interest in me because of this, so be it. I love you but would rather lose you than lose myself."*

When your boundaries are respected, you are respected. You feel heard and seen.

When they are not respected, you feel resentful, anxious, stressed, confused and unsafe.

Good, respected boundaries = healthy relationships.

Relationship Mindset

No one can rescue me, save me, complete me, change me or make me happy but me.

We are not responsible for each other's emotions.

Drama is not interesting. There is no jealousy, wrath, abuse, blame, grand gestures or emotional addiction.

We set clear boundaries, and respect the boundaries of the other.

We both work at identifying our expectations and our assumptions.

The more clearly we communicate, the better our partnership.

We are open about the things that hurt us.

We are invested in (rather than afraid of) the growth and evolution of the other.

We are OK with being uncomfortable.

We are OK with things being awkward.

We understand that triggers are something to work through, not something to run from.

We understand it's normal to feel attraction towards others.

We do not attempt to control, manipulate, own, dominate the other.

We keep our word: to ourselves and to each other.

We both benefit from independence.

We both want and need time alone.

Do You Have Healthy Boundaries?

My boundaries are pretty solid.

My boundaries are a catastrophe.

In some ways my boundaries are very healthy. I have learned to say no. I can easily present my case. I step away from over-explaining something I don't really need to give explanations for. All these things used to be hard for me, but they are getting easier and easier.

In other ways my boundaries need so much work. I often feel responsible for the well-being of others, or how they feel. I have an urge to step in and try to fix whatever they are struggling with, which often ends up making me feel like I'm giving more than I should. This pattern leaves me feeling exhausted and often heartbroken, which basically means I exhaust myself, and break my own heart.

I work very hard at stepping away from the notion that I am valuable or lovable because I can help.

I don't have any tattoos but maybe I need one across my heart that reminds me I cannot save another. I can only save myself.

How Do You Distinguish
Love From Despair?

Love and despair have nothing to do with each other. Love is present, solid, healthy, has boundaries. Despair is the opposite of confidence. It breeds carelessness, frenzy, haste. It is urgent, foolhardy, impetuous.

His back is to the wall.

If someone is desperate, his ability to discern is compromised. There is an absence of boundaries.

Without these things, neither he nor I know who he is.

I can't be in a relationship if I cannot see whom it is that I am loving.

Is It Okay to Let Friends Violate My Personal Space?

Some time ago I got certified to be a yoga teacher. As a teacher, sometimes I walk up to students and adjust their pose for optimum alignment. This means I put my hands on their body.

Many people love being adjusted or touched. Many people do not want it.

Let me take it a step further. Many people who love being adjusted and touched have days when they don't want to.

In other words, just because I have always touched them does not mean I always can.

Each individual has his or her boundaries. I cannot fudge them, negotiate them, argue them, push back on them. I cannot require or demand an explanation.

Before I touch, I ask.

Your boundaries — even when they move, even when they change, even when they are seemingly capricious and inconstant — are your boundaries. You don't ever need to justify, explain, elaborate or rationalize.

They belong to you and as such they can be anything you want.

How Do You Set Boundaries in a Relationship?

Get clear on what you want and what you don't.

Get comfortable disappointing others. Getting approval for another to like you is the enemy of a clear boundary.

Understand that having boundaries is healthy, not selfish.

Say yes or no devoid of ambivalence.

Listen to others so you respect their boundaries too. Respect begets respect (or should).

Remember: if it's your body or your property, you decide. You are the boss. *"No, I don't want sex tonight."*

If it's another person's body or property, that is not a boundary, that is controlling. *"If you don't have sex with me tonight..."*

Boundaries are not static. They change, so you have to be attuned to what you want and what the people around you are comfortable with.

What Does 'Deal-Breaker' Mean?

A deal-breaker is something you are not willing to negotiate.

If you dream of getting married and the person you are dating says marriage is not in their plans, this could be a deal-breaker.

If one of you wants children and the other does not, one of you will have to give up something that will impact the rest of your life.

If one of you is monogamous and the other is not, the relationship is destined to be painful and fraught with conflict.

A deal-breaker is often a way of saying *"there is nothing wrong with who you are and nothing wrong with who I am but there is a fundamental lack of compatibility here and compromising will cost us our happiness."*

Other types of big deal-breakers are less about incompatibility and more about basic boundaries related to self-esteem: *if you yell at me, threaten me, call me names or ever strike me in anger there is no coming back from that.*

Unannounced

I had a friend who used to drop in unannounced. The first time it happened I felt mildly imposed upon but pleased to see her. After that I felt like diving under the bed but pretended I was happy about her unplanned arrivals.

I want to be a good person. I want to be generous. I want to do right by my friends. I want them to feel supported by me.

It's maybe for these reasons that I waited until I felt desperate. By that point I was angry, resentful, feeling like I was being taken advantage of.

If you wait until you're at the end of your rope to handle something like this, you come at it when any reservoir of patience or grace has run out.

Boundaries are not, *"Hey, you have gone too far."* Ideally they mean, *"This is the line. Please remain on the other side so that you going too far does not happen."*

Are Boundaries Selfish?

The Best of Me

It's so hard to attempt to change for another.

It's easy to feel you are compromising yourself.

When the dynamics of a relationship are pushing me to change, I ask myself one thing.

Who is it that I want to be?

Do I want, for example, to be petty, insecure, nagging, demanding, rapacious? Do I want to feel in the cavity of my chest a tightening, a grasping, despair? Do I want to live with the acerbity that arises from trying unsuccessfully to make another person do what I think they should do?

Or do I want to feel increasingly free, expansive, independent; clear on my own pursuits and interests, strong?

I don't change for others. I change for myself.

This means that every opportunity to love is also an opportunity for me to become a better person, to exercise my character in a new way.

I don't become resentful because whatever it is that I decide to do I am doing it for me.

This isn't selfish. It's giving.

Give others the best of you.

Used

Feeling used was so painful I had to dissect it.

What I found was I always played a role in it.

Offering something to another person cultivates dependency. If I can make you need me, that will keep you close.

This is how I discovered that being used was a form of manipulation — to the exact same degree as using someone.

I stopped feeling sorry for myself when I understood that the person being used feels like a victim but instead holds the power. The person doing the using feels shrewd but is at the mercy of the victim deciding to acquiesce.

Today, if any relationship I am in seems to lack symmetry — a delicate, sensitive equilibrium that feels healthy and true — if someone looks me up only if they need me, or things feel unbalanced in a way that tugs or pulls at me, I step away.

The "you are using me" dynamic needs two willing, active parties in order to survive. If either party refuses to engage, being used becomes a thing of your past.

Why Does My Boyfriend Keep Cheating on Me?

One of the "life lessons" I learn and then forget and have to keep re-learning, over and over, is that I have no control over the actions of others. If only I could do something to change their behavior my problems would be fixed — except, there is nothing I can do to change another person's behavior.

The formula that helps is to remind myself to turn the desired action back to me. I can't tell others what to do, but I can tell me what to do.

Applying this formula to your question becomes — *Why do I stay with someone who keeps cheating on me?*

Life-Long Exercise

Let's pretend I have a dark secret.

I believe I am not good enough and therefore I operate under that assumption.

I am convinced that in order to deserve love I have to please others.

I have to work at getting people to like me.

If someone else wants anything from me I am compelled to provide it. Otherwise, they won't want to be with me.

Examples of what other people might want from me vary broadly: help with their homework, keeping their secrets, liking what they like, wanting to do what they want to do. Sex.

I'm almost pleading at first. I jump at the chance to give what I can.

But then, wait a minute. This isn't right.

I feel used, become resentful, angry.

Resentment is an indication of poor boundaries. I shouldn't have let it get this far.

Another symptom of poor boundaries is the sense something is wrong with "everybody."

Why is everybody using me? Why does everyone lie to me? Why does everyone end up betraying me?

Boundaries are hard to set — saying no is difficult — because the underlying belief is that saying no will cost me the relationship. It is an indication that I am not giving enough, that I am not loyal enough, not dedicated enough.

It must mean I'm selfish.

But setting boundaries is not selfish. It's healthy. It's how I respect myself.

Look around you. Boundaries are why fences exist, and walls and doors and curtains. They are indispensable for our well-being.

I need to honor myself enough to acknowledge that my boundaries can and will shift. They are mine, so they can do anything they want.

Yesterday I was happy to help you with your homework. I am not willing to do it today. I had sex with you last night. I don't want to this morning. I don't have to explain.

Boundary setting is a life-long exercise that you often need to re-examine, re-establish. *I am giving up my weekend to finish what my boss asked me to do. I'm working late, again.*

I'm saying yes when I want to say no to get someone to think well of me.

I need to be brave enough to say: *This is who I am. This is what I like. This is what I can do for you. But, you can't push against who I am. You can't get me to like something I don't.*

You can't get me to do anything that makes me uncomfortable.

My discomfort for your benefit is not healthy for either of us.

How Do I Set Boundaries During the COVID-19 Pandemic?

It's so very hard to set boundaries.

Put simply, setting boundaries makes me feel like I'm putting my relationships at risk. But, setting boundaries is healthy, it's necessary, and now, in the middle of a global pandemic, essential to my health.

Setting boundaries is how I love myself.

Boundaries sound like:

I love you very much but I am not comfortable going to a bar right now.

That sounds like so much fun but it makes me feel like I'm taking a risk I'm not ready for.

I completely understand what you are saying. I don't think it's worth it to take that risk right now.

I want to see you in person but I don't think it's a good idea. This of course is unrelated to how I feel about you.

Things to avoid:

Your boundaries are for you and about you. This means setting a boundary does not involve the other person. For example: *"I need some time to inform myself to see if the socially distant activity you are suggesting is actually safe"* is different from *"I need you to stop making suggestions that put me at risk."*

You do not need to explain yourself or apologize for your boundaries. It's important to be kind and courteous, but explaining too much begins to sound like I am defending or justifying myself and this is a huge, unnecessary expenditure of energy, and opens the door for the boundary to be pushed or tested.

You might want to include what you will do if the boundary is repeatedly crossed. *"I value our friendship so much but if you keep reaching out to insist that we hang out I won't be responding to your messages."*

Losing Yourself

If you have a tendency to lose yourself in a relationship, when you are single you feel like you are in a state of suspension. Looking. Expectant.

Without a relationship, but also when you've been in one for long enough, you begin to feel purposeless, like you're moving through the motions but something is not quite in its place.

You are not your own priority, because *"that would be selfish."*

You define yourself and estimate your own worth in the function of the role you play — how "helpful" you are, how "useful", how others "can't live without" whatever you do for them. It's hard for you to arrive at the notion that you don't need to "do" anything to be loved.

You can't make decisions without consulting with him, even if this decision does not impact him but has a huge impact on you.

Your significant other is your everything, your best friend. He is your soul mate. He completes you. This language is the language of fairy tales, and in real life the language of codependency.

You worry. You feel anxious. This angst means you try to control another's behavior in an attempt to manage your own off the rails emotions. *"Don't come home too late or I can't sleep."*

You need another person to do things for you that you should know how to do for yourself. Calm yourself. Comfort yourself. Understand, listen to and sort through your feelings.

You don't know if that is your opinion or his opinion and you answer questions about what you do and what you like with "we" — never "me."

You can't plan anything without planning with him.

You can't answer simple questions. Who are you? What do you want? What do you like? It's not that the answers are a work in progress. It's that you are drawing a blank.

You stop doing things that are for you or that were once important to you.

You never spend time any with yourself. If you do, you are not with you. You are waiting. You check your phone 386 times. Clearly this indicates how important he is to you.

When choosing between anything and your significant other you choose spending time with your significant other. You believe this is because you love him. I mean, there is nothing you'd rather be doing, so why not?

One day you wake up to realize just how many things you've lost: what happened to the trip you meant to take, the class you were planning to enroll in, the interests you were going to explore? What happened to your friends?

You break up and it doesn't feel like you've lost a person. It feels like you've lost everything.

When You're Not Ruled by Ego

I am able to hear something my ego says (*Dushka, this is personal! This is about you!* or *Oh my god everyone is better than me!*) and recognize it as a story rather than as a fact.

My ego begins to make fewer decisions for me.

As such, I begin to notice and shift my patterns.

I don't need to convince anyone about anything.

I realize that how people behave is a reflection of them, not a reflection of me. (This means that what someone else does cannot be the measure of my worth.)

Being misunderstood no longer makes me feel like I am alone.

I realize I cannot control, save, fix, improve or change anyone but me. This is liberating.

Conversely, I get better at setting boundaries. Taking care of myself has become more important than compromising myself in an attempt to manage how you feel about me.

I seldom feel resentful since resentment feels like I am angry at someone else but is instead a sign that I have disrespected my boundaries.

I begin looking beyond the labels I typically use to define myself. (*Yah I may be an introvert but I'm also quite social so maybe we are more than one thing?*)

What I Learned From Lois

I have a friend named Jacob who has two older sisters.

His mom, Lois, was an angel. Generous, loving, attentive. She lived for her kids and gave them everything — her time, her attention, her things.

They were used to the fact that whatever was hers was theirs.

One day, when all the kids were in their very early teens, the whole family went to a restaurant for lunch.

Lois looked at all of these people that she loved so much, and declared *"I'm going to order fries. I'm not going to share them. They are all for me. So, if anyone wants fries, please order your own".*

First, total disbelief. I mean, she must be kidding.

When the fries arrived, she pulled the plate over to her own space (instead of what she usually did, which was push it to the center of the table) and squirted mustard on them.

Denial. *"What are you doing, Mom!? We don't like mustard!"*

She slowly dipped a fry in the mustard, placed it into her mouth, and chewed it.

Indignation. Anger.

"Mom! Just pass the fries! What is happening?"

Outrage. *"This is so unfair!"*

Crunch. Dip. Munch.

Accusations. *"Mom! This is so selfish! What's gotten into you?! This is not like you!"*

Assumptions. *"Did we do something? Are you mad at us?"*

They glared. They squirmed. She calmly finished her fries.

"Children," she said, wiping her mouth. *"I have not had my very own plate of anything for over a decade. I've decided I don't like sharing my fries."*

It's difficult for people to recognize boundaries because they are thinking of themselves, of what they want, what is convenient for them, or even what they are used to. They are not thinking of you.

It's difficult because boundaries change, day by day, and sometimes not for a decade.

But if you enforce them with love, then you get whatever it is you need to put yourself in a position to keep on giving.

How Much Should I Give Up for My Relationship?

Codependency is defined as neglecting myself to accommodate someone else — giving up my boundaries in an effort to be seen, approved of, or be lovable.

In the beginning of a romantic relationship, this self-neglect does not feel like a sacrifice. It feels natural, even joyful and generous. *Yes, please. Let me give myself over to you.*

It feels like this is what I know how to do, what I'm supposed to do. *This is what love is. I want to be good at loving you.*

I tell you I like things I don't really care for. I abandon my interests to spend more time with you. I cancel dates with my friends for us.

I need alone time but give it up to fill my afternoons with you.

I am neglecting myself because it feels so good, like I have become effervescent. And, because it would be selfish not to. I am putting us first — us before me.

It feels like taking a hit from the best drug the world has ever known.

It's only later that I realize that the outlines of me are being erased, and that I'm the one responsible for the erasing.

Do I know myself? What do I like? What do I want?

If it feels like I need you to do things I should be doing for myself — *I can't breathe without you, I can't live without you, I can't be happy without you, I can't make important decisions without you, I can't run my life without you, I can't get through Sunday without you* — then the inevitable fate of the relationship is that I will suffocate it.

In a healthy relationship I establish boundaries early. I defend them, even when it feels lackluster, boring or counterintuitive.

I recognize some of these boundaries as elastic. But the fact that I am not being rigid about what matters to me doesn't mean I betray everything, blow past all of it in the name of us.

I have the discipline, the rigor, to put myself first, not because it's selfish but because I can't love you well if along the way I forget who I am.

Incompatible

If you and another person are "incompatible" it means you cannot happily live together.

It does not mean you are not *"open to change"* or that you are not *"willing to put in the work".*

It often means you are absolutely, intensely wanting, fighting, struggling to make it work — all you want is for this to just work — but you cannot get there from here.

Relinquishing a characteristic that makes you incompatible feels like you are compromising not just your happiness but your identity.

If one of you is punctual and the other always late, you can negotiate a somewhat incongruous life with its own brand of rhythm.

But what if one of you is monogamous and the other polyamorous? What if one of you places a great deal of importance in material things and the other does not assign meaning to money? What if one is a systemic liar and the other requires honesty in order to function? What if one is deeply insecure and the other repeatedly hurt by being constantly doubted?

Is changing to meet your relationship's demands making you a better person? Is it stretching you, contributing to your growth?

Or is it forcing you to be someone other than who you are?

Hot Tea

Once, sipping tea with my dad, I took a gulp of boiling hot liquid. He was looking at me when this happened and instantly — before I could instinctively swallow — he barked an order. *"Spit that out."* I did.

Afterward I felt ashamed. We were in a very fancy restaurant.

"Dushka," he said. *"It's better to be embarrassed than to scald your mouth and your esophagus. Your well-being first. Social norms second."*

Over the years I have considered what a metaphor this is to life. Have you ever put yourself in harm's way to avoid being rude? Have you ever been unclear with your boundaries to avoid hurting someone's feelings?

Your well-being first. Social norms second.

How Do You Fix Yourself in a Relationship?

Relationships are a very good place for me to quickly identify what it is that I need to work on.

We can make a pact to support each other's evolution.

I can commit to my own health and well-being and feel supported by someone with similar commitments to himself.

With my significant other, I can work on boundaries: what they are, how it feels to enforce them.

I can practice communicating as clearly as possible.

I can practice being vulnerable, talk about how things make you feel.

I can become aware of the things I do to try to control another person and begin learning how to work on myself instead of blaming or manipulating.

We can both work together through triggers (in loving relationships it's common to have a knack for pushing each other's buttons).

Finally, I want to say I don't agree with the word "fix". There is nothing to fix. I am not broken. I am whole and capable of growth. This is also true for you.

This evolution puts us in a place where we are responsible, accountable, can work on ourselves and consequently suffer less.

Do You Find It Easy to Say "No"?

I find it easy to say no when it comes to something I don't want to do. (For example, turning down an invitation to a birthday party.)

I find it very difficult not to volunteer a yes when the yes is none of my business. I always want to help. I always feel that doing something about what another person is struggling with is my responsibility.

This is not a generous trait. It's invasive, disguised as generous, and it takes constant work for me to hold back.

I am perpetually whispering to myself *"You don't need to fix or help or assist others. They don't need you to swoop in and meddle. What they need is for you to grant them the space to figure it out on their own."*

We all have our battles.

What Are Some Examples
of Poor Boundaries?

Poor boundaries aren't evil. Most of the time they don't imply ill intent. They imply self-ignorance, a disconnect with yourself.

Poor boundaries are a sign you have compromised yourself or are (often inadvertently) infringing upon the boundaries of others.

You are responsible for you.

The other person is responsible for him or herself.

Anything that breaches this very basic frontier between where you end and others begin is a display of poor boundaries.

One way to tell if you have poor boundaries is if there seems to be something wrong with the whole entire world:

Why am I so nice? Everyone takes advantage of me.

Why isn't anybody helping me?

If I don't do everything around here it doesn't get done right.

Why doesn't anyone understand me?

Why isn't anybody saving me?

Why are there no good men/women left?

Why is everyone so selfish?

Why am I always in the middle of so much drama?

Another symptom of poor boundaries is resentment. Are you angry at another person because you find yourself doing something you didn't want to to do? That's code for you being angry with yourself.

In your relationships, the arrow that points straight to poor boundaries is that you feel something and expect your feelings to impact the actions of another person.

I'm sorry to report that your feelings = your actions.

This holds true even when it's all wrapped up in love.

That looks like this:

I'm cold. Put a sweater on.

I love you. You need to do what I need you to do so I can feel safe.

I love you unconditionally.

This is love at first sight and I think we should get married.

I love you. This clearly means you love me.

I am a selfless hero who really wants to help you, save you, rescue you, fix you, improve you.

You need me.

I need you.

Please don't eat that. You're on a diet.

I forbid you to smoke. It's bad for you.

I am a jealous person. You can't have women friends.

You can't go to a party without me.

You belong to me.

Another display of poor boundaries manifests in unreasonable demands on yourself. Your brain does not respect your body. And your body is you.

Your body is telling you what it needs, then pleading with you, and then making you sick so that you finally slow down and listen. That looks like this:

I am so very busy. I don't have time for my family or for friends because I'm very, very important.

I stay up all night working and I have so much work. When will it end?

I need to be alone sometimes but don't want to hurt the people that I love.

I just don't think needing alone time is really a thing.

Resting makes me feel guilty. So does napping and doing nothing.

Any version of taking care of myself makes me feel selfish.

Any version of doing something for pleasure or just because feels like a waste of time.

Why do I always get sick when I have important things going on?

Why do I feel so tired?

The creation of good boundaries is really hard and takes constant practice.

As your boundaries become clearer and firmer, so does your self-esteem.

Money

A friend once called and asked to borrow money from me. I said no.

My friend spends beyond her means and owes many people money.

I love her, am always happy to lend her my ear and take her to lunch, and think it would be a shame to allow money to affect our friendship.

I trust her completely. I trust her to be exactly who she is.

If at any point she (or anyone else) perceives my refusal to lend a friend money as "selfish", I am not too concerned.

It's so easy to confuse the concept of "selflessness" with what is actually better defined as poor boundaries.

If I am repeatedly manipulated or targeted, this does not mean I am "too nice".

It means my boundaries are unclear.

This trait is destructive, affects my ability to establish healthy relationships and is unrelated to a generosity of spirit.

Has Focusing on You Ever Improved Your Relationship?

Imagine for a moment that I am needy. I need company. I need frequent reassurance. I want texts to be responded to at a certain cadence. I want to hear you say *"I love you"*.

I end up in a relationship with someone emotionally distant. He does not need to see me every day, is not in the habit of looking at his phone, and he already told me he loves me and thinks it's smarmy to say it all the time.

I can focus on him. I can talk to him, tell him I need his attention, explain how what he is failing to do makes me feel.

Or I can focus on me. I can ask myself how this neediness is making me feel, so desperate and grasping. I can ask myself how it's served me in the past. I can ask myself if this is the person I want to be. I can learn how to evolve out of needing, not for him, but for me.

In my personal experience, focusing on myself is the only thing that has ever improved my relationships.

Attached

When I was a teenager my boyfriend (not a specific boyfriend — any boyfriend) was my life. I wanted to talk to him and be with him and I willingly allowed everything else to fade into the background.

What I mean by "everything else" was me.

I quickly went from involved and in love to needy. To second guessing myself. *Should I do this? Should I stop? Does he think of me? Does he miss me? Does he love me?*

My love became grasping and desperate even when I knew I needed to hold what I loved gently, loosely, on an open palm.

Squeezing that hand kills the delicate thing you are holding.

The antidote to this predicament was not in him. It was not in him telling me to call him less or call him more. Not in him saying I was too intense or not intense enough. Not in him deciding that I was or was not too much.

It was not even in him calling me as much as I called him.

The antidote was in putting more attention, not less, in all the things I had once so willingly allowed to fade into the background: my life, my interests, my friends, myself.

The antidote was in recognizing that this desperate grasping person was not who I wanted to be, and that to stop the person I needed to fall in love with was me.

How Do I Get My Girlfriend to Stop Eating From My Plate?

My mother and I love to share our food. We gently orchestrate what others order so we can taste everything.

My brother does not like sharing his food. He wants other people's forks away from his plate even when he doesn't want what's on it anymore.

We really did not like this at all. *Why aren't you ordering what we are suggesting? Don't you see that our way means you can taste more things? And, why can't you learn to share? What an outrage. Don't be selfish.*

But, you know what? The plate of his food is his. Not wanting to share is his right.

He needed to come to terms with the fact that his decision would make us protest, would make us try to get him to see the error of his ways. He needed to get us to respect what was rightfully his.

One day, he ordered his very own dish (not what we suggested he order). Before his plate arrived he looked at us. *"I ordered what I want to eat and I want to tell you I am not going to share it. I love you, but whatever is on my plate is mine and not available to you."*

103

Today, my mom and I decide together what we will jointly order and taste each other's food. We leave my brother out of it. Sometimes, when his dish arrives and looks delicious, we sulk. He holds his ground. You should too.

What Is Something You Sacrificed for Your Partner?

For 15 years I was married to a man I also worked with.

We were incredibly compatible, completely in love, and wonderful collaborators. For the duration of our relationship we were together 24 hours a day.

During that time I was preposterously happy. In many ways my life was effortless. I had an accomplice, I felt loved and supported, and simply put, made my husband my priority.

If you had asked me then where the center of the planet was I would have told you it was under the soles of his feet.

Through the years, we both sacrificed "me" to become "we".

Somewhere along the way we lost ourselves.

After 15 years our relationship imploded without drama or ceremony. We felt listless, trapped. There was no fight, no big incident, no betrayal, no transgression — but the absence of a "me" in both of us created a vacuum we did not know how to fill.

A sacrifice is, by definition, the giving up of something valuable. It implies a tough, mostly internal decision, perhaps an offering. We were not making a sacrifice as much as loving each other in the best way we knew how.

If I could turn back time, I would change nothing.

That said, to this day I wonder what it says about me that I am so quick, so willing to totally relinquish something as sacred as my sovereignty in the name of love.

My marriage taught me that if you give up who you are there is no one left for the other person to love, and no one left to do the loving.

Bad Houseguest

A friend once asked if she could stay at my house for a short period of time. I don't like sharing my private space and said yes in an attempt to be nice.

Once she arrived she took over — she filled my closets with her things, had boxes of stuff in my living room, seemed to inhabit every room I walked into.

She took me at my word when I suggested she make herself at home.

A few weeks in I realized I was telling her to do the very opposite of what I wanted. I had done this to myself.

With newfound clarity, I went into the kitchen and told her it was time for her to leave.

She looked startled and asked if she could have some time to get her things together. I told her I needed my space back and that the best I could do was give her until nightfall. Then I left the house.

When I got back, my place felt vast and quiet. I could breathe in it again. I spent a full week reclaiming my territory, washing towels and sheets, straightening things out, moving furniture. I had the house cleaned, the windows washed. I opened them wide.

I love my friends. I love my family. The best thing I can do for my relationships is accept the person that I am. I am a person who does not share her private, sacred space.

I donated the bed in the guest room, bought a desk and set a vase of flowers on it. Then, I declared it my home office.

I decided then and there I would not be needing it as a guest room again.

Confidence

If I could talk to a younger version of myself I would tell her that confidence doesn't happen despite anxiety but because of it.

Anxiety is part of who I am, and loving myself begins with accepting all of me, angst and all.

I would also tell her that there is nothing stable, composed or consistent about confidence. Both confidence and identity are like everything else: they fluctuate.

I'm in a perpetual state of flux, and so are you.

It's really important to step into a virtuous circle of choices and decisions that are good for me. Not to look good to someone else, but to be as strong and healthy as I can be, for me.

These choices and decisions are not a symptom of loving myself — they are the path to loving myself.

I would recognize how much I crave approval and praise and patiently practice looking within for motivation, inspiration and drive. I don't want to rely on anything erratic that I cannot control. (I do not crave approval and praise any less: it's that approval and praise do not guide the decisions that I make.)

I would distance myself from anything I know is not good for me. From people who play games to a job where I'm not learning to anything I know is unsatisfactory.

I also think deeply about the fact that toxicity and mediocrity are a system, and that I need to work on myself to detect, then end the ways I contribute.

I stop exerting effort to get anyone to love me or be interested in me. Few things extinguish my confidence as much as this. Nothing dries out my soul more than the effort of convincing someone I am worth loving. I want the people in my life to be as interested in me as I am in them. This will alter my relationship landscape.

I'd make time to pursue the things that interest me, that engage me. My creative endeavors are where I should be putting my time and my attention. They are what I have to contribute to the world.

Perhaps most importantly, I would challenge any hint of a thought that suggests putting myself first is selfish. This is how we love better: with the best, strongest, most examined version of us, not the one who feels small, scattered, helpless, worthless, needy.

It's Supposed to Work Like This

Feeling loved because I am and not because I do.

Love that feels like support and not like dependency.

A relationship that feels like fulfillment and not needy or convenient.

A sense that I have an ally, rather than a transaction, arrangement or quid pro quo.

Boundaries, instead of resentment; accountability over myself instead of nagging the other.

Feeling seen instead of feeling taken for granted.

A freedom from feeling responsible over things I could never control.

Feeling like I'm in a safe space rather than playing games.

A sense of self-worth instead of constant fear of being abandoned.

An understanding of the other as fallible instead of expecting perfection.

My Mom's Husband Is Mean to Me

If I wanted to see my mom and she was married to someone who was mean to me I would talk to her.

I would tell her everything — that I love her, that I want to spend time with her, that I don't know what to do.

I would very calmly tell her about her husband and how he makes me feel.

I would want her to make room for me — to find a way to spend time with me without this meaning I have to spend time with him.

I would be very clear on establishing my boundaries: I stay away from people who are mean to me, as well as from people who make me uncomfortable.

I would hear her out. I would listen and keep an open mind to whatever she proposes.

That being said, I'd be careful about compromising what I need to do to keep myself both safe and comfortable.

One or the Other

I love to write. I always have. And yet throughout my life my writing has been intermittent. It has never stopped but I have diminished it down to a trickle.

This is because I am an all-in sort of person, enthusiastic and extreme. When I enter a relationship I give it all I've got — my attention and my time. My intention and my energy. My focus and my determination.

I want to do things right.

Writing takes a lot. It is very time consuming and takes grit and discipline.

Oh, look. It takes the very same things a relationship requires.

So it was one or the other. *No, Dushka. You can't have both. You don't have the space, and you don't have the time.*

It took me decades to realize that what I was giving to my relationship was precisely what was killing it: I was suffocating it with my intensity and my vehemence.

And my writing? My writing was always there waiting for me. It did not ever require that I struggle to carefully modulate how much of me to give it. My writing could take me whole.

I don't know if losing yourself in a relationship is "normal." I've never been an authority on what that word actually means. I do know that it's common, and that it's a mistake.

You lose yourself willingly with the choices that you make, and one day the person your significant other fell in love with is no longer there.

How Do You Tell a Guest They Have to Go?

You have no idea how uncomfortable it makes me to have people in my space.

For years this made me feel like I was a terrible person. Like I was selfish and didn't know how to share. It took me a long time to accept that the place where I live belongs to me and I am happiest when I don't have anyone over.

When I do have people over it's because they are very close to me and know me well. They know I am doing something for them that I don't do for everyone.

We visit for a bit and then I begin nervously glancing at the door. This is usually enough, but when it isn't, I stand up and say *"Thank you so much for coming over. It's time for you to go".*

And they do.

Why Are Boundaries Hard?

Proud of Me

One morning many years ago, my Dad, my two younger brothers and I were having breakfast.

"Some day," my father told one of my brothers, *"you will be a doctor."*

"What about me?" said the other.

"You," my Dad said with a smile *"will be a lawyer."*

"And me?" I asked.

"You," he said anointing me, *"you are going to be the mother of my grandchildren."*

I imagine this conversation, taken out of context and out of time, would spark outrage. But my father loved me. This was his dream.

Back then, his words filled my chest. Someday my children would run in his garden and sit with him in his library.

Except, that never happened. I went to work and loved it: the challenge, the discipline, the variety, the demands. I got married quite young and got a divorce less than a year later.

If I could summarize the trajectory of life I'd say that things do not turn out the way you plan them, and that this is the best part.

It's where the astonishment is, the awe and the gratitude.

Along the rocky way you will disappoint so many people, in particular the people who love you the most, including yourself. This is the mark of a life that belongs only to you.

Despite any temporary delusion, the fact is you are never obligated to do anything you might believe you are supposed to do.

You possess the greatest gift bestowed on humankind: free will.

You can but don't have to find a significant other, a house, have a wedding, have children. These are all options that work for a few people but not for others.

(Anecdotally, I had a wonderful significant other and a beautiful house and a loving wedding only to realize I wasn't happy and wanted none of it.)

In one of the great paradoxes of life, no matter what you do everyone will judge you and nobody will care.

For both of these reasons what others think about your choices should not be given much consideration.

I buried my father last year. I never gave him any of the things he wanted for me.

I can tell you without a doubt that for everything I am and everything I have done, for every choice I made, every mistake, every flaw, every shortcoming, he was incalculably, inestimably, recklessly proud of me.

How Can I Stop Disappointing My Parents?

What my father wanted more than anything was grandchildren.

Do you know that deep yearning women feel, to be mothers? That calling?

I never felt that.

When I was a little girl I thought maybe that sensation would come later. I took for granted that when I got old enough I would find my soul mate, get pregnant, become a mother, and make my father a granddad.

I did eventually meet a wonderful man, and we talked about having children and just weren't sure. Someday, we said. Sure — someday. Just not now.

My friends began having children and I could see the kind of commitment and dedication being a parent actually was. It felt wrong for me — so wrong.

The fact that it felt wrong felt terrifying.

I had never considered I would never be somebody's mom. I had never thought it possible that I would not give my father what he wanted the most.

But, wait a minute.

If I had a child, who would live with the consequences of this decision? Whose life would be forever altered?

My father would be involved maybe once a week.

The life completely transformed would be mine.

On one of the many times he asked me *"When, Dushka? When are you going to tell me you are expecting my grandchild?"* I finally said *"Dad, I don't think that's ever going to happen. I am so sorry, but I don't want children."*

He stared at me. He frowned. Then he smiled. *"Well,"* he said. *"They are kind of a pain. They never do what you think they will. It's like they are their own people."*

This is the most representative example of a time where I disappointed one of my parents. There were many others, both big and small: I was not a good student, I kept secrets, I did not go to a fancy college, I did not become a lawyer, I did not become an artist, I married a guy they didn't think was right for me, my hair was always unruly, I got a divorce, I did not change the world.

The summary is this — every time I disappointed them I chose to fully step into the fact that my life is mine and mine alone.

Disappointing people — your parents, your family, your friends and sometimes yourself — is necessary if you want to fully become the person you were meant to.

I hope you never stop disappointing your parents. I hope that with time it becomes less painful. And I hope that in doing so you fall in love with the incredible stranger who lives inside of you.

Does Being Compliant Make You Happier?

The word "compliant" implies submission, obeying. It means I am "manageable", which I guess might make someone else's life happier and easier, but not mine.

I am not suggesting I need to be unyielding or rigid. But I am a human with needs and interests and I take up space. Acting docile does not make my life easier. It makes me resentful and angry. It makes me feel like I don't exist.

Deep inside wanting to be loved, wanting to belong, there is something feral inside me that refuses to be dominated. I can live an easy, happy life as long as I respect others, and others respect me.

How Do You Spot a Narcissist?

The word "narcissism" is in vogue. In fashion. It's trendy. It's easy to use as a shorthand, an automatic way to point to someone and imply *"everything was his fault"*.

Narcissism is a personality disorder. This means it's not to be confused with someone who is merely egocentric, selfish or self-involved. Narcissism is more serious than that.

A narcissist regards himself as a god. *I mean, believe me, nobody is better at that than me. Nobody.*

A narcissist does not feel empathy. He does not concern himself with others — just himself. He will organize his world so that he receives constant adulation. He has admirers and fans but not friends.

He is convinced that the law and consideration that applies to the rest of the world does not apply to him. He will not change, because he can't.

Any criticism, no matter how trite, will infuriate a narcissist. We instead need to understand how privileged we are to have him in our life.

Narcissists destroy the world around them. This is because they have no notion of the consequences of their actions.

124

If you are in the company of a narcissist, stop asking what you can do to change him, or how you can make coexistence possible. Instead, turn the question on yourself.

Why am I in a relationship without healthy boundaries? Why is it OK to live only to fawn over another? Why did I choose a person who would feel threatened by the mere fact that I have my own identity?

You cannot change another person, but you can work on yourself. This is particularly true in a relationship with someone convinced we are honored by the fact he walks among us.

What's 'Enmeshment' and How Does It Affect Families?

A boundary is a way of saying *"this is where you end and I begin"*.

Enmeshment is a tangle. It's the word you use when boundaries don't exist, are unclear, or are constantly pushed on and disrespected.

If boundaries are not clear, relationships are impaired. If I am sad because you are sad, I cannot support you. If I am so involved in your life that your experiences are my experiences, we can blame each other for the choices we make and feel resentful instead of accountable. Things that are healthy and marks of sovereignty feel like a form of betrayal.

Some signs of enmeshment:

Privacy is non-existent. (The fact is there is nothing wrong with not feeling like telling someone everything.)

Someone in the family wants to control the other.

I feel it's my job to keep someone else's secrets.

An inability to say no. Because, you can't say no to family. (Yes. Yes you can.)

A sense that we are responsible for how the other feels or acts which in turn makes me feel valuable and loved.

A conviction that it's my job to mediate, fix or manage dynamics that don't involve me.

Taking care of another in a way that results in total neglect of myself.

Family enmeshment — which in turn leads to a pattern of codependency in my relationships outside of family — is incredibly common mostly because members of our family are inexpert and human and repeat what they know.

The antidote to enmeshment is the creation and the protection of boundaries. This is really hard because when people are enmeshed, boundaries feel like a form of treason.

Enforce them anyway.

What Aspect Did You Change That Made Things Better?

I went from a pattern of codependency to learning how to love myself.

It's not so much that I didn't love myself before — rather, that my entire life gravitated around the person that I loved, making me forget about myself.

I realized this invariably led to relationships that were not healthy, and that what we learn to call "mad, romantic, undying, unconditional love" is actually an absence of boundaries that never ends well.

I stepped away from things that hurt me and put into place habits that would improve things for me over time.

I took responsibility and ownership of anything that affected my vital space, learned to disappoint others, to say no, and to create my own sacred ceremonies.

Over time this had an impact over all my relationships. I lost a few people — in particular those who were comfortable with me making sacrifices that hurt me and benefited them. People who wanted what was best for me stayed, or became closer, better friends.

I don't think loving myself is an act or a sudden change but rather something I practice. Sometimes (more than sometimes) I overextend myself, forget to establish boundaries or dive off the deep end into a dynamic that ends up compromising me. What's changed is that I'm more aware of it, notice it sooner and course correct.

I can't recommend this enough.

Should I Delete a Friend From Social Media?

I spend a lot of time on social media. It's a creative outlet for me and my writing, and a way to connect with others.

How social media makes me feel has a huge impact on my life.

Controlling what affects me is a form of self-care.

I scroll through my feed and notice. How does this make me feel? Happy, connected, purposeful, inspired? Or does it make me feel pain, left out, isolated, in a constant state of frenzy, like I'm missing something?

Why is this person showing up on my feed? Is it obsessive and hurtful? Is it healthy? Is it keeping me from moving on?

Is it interfering with me noticing everything that's good about my life?

I have many tools available to me to remove someone from my feed. Things don't need to be drastic or fraught with drama. I can mute, unfollow, unfriend, block. I can make decisions for now that I can change later.

Is it a good idea to delete your friend from social media? I don't know. How is seeing her social media posts making you feel?

What Expectations Do People Need to Drop?

An expectation is the version of another person that we have imagined.

By definition, having any expectation is the reason we feel disappointment: we disappoint ourselves.

I Can't Live if Living Is Without Me

Tell me, I was saying. *Tell me who it is you want me to be.*

Just please don't leave me.

We think it's romantic — even required — to change who we are in the name of love.

Everything we have been taught about love is wrong.

Through fairy tales and music and movies we are bombarded by consistent notions about what love is: *I can't live if living is without you.*

And we say implausible things in the name of love: *I will do anything for you. I need you. I cannot live without you. You are my everything.*

You complete me.

These concepts are not evidence of true love. They are evidence of desperation and dependency. They sow unhealthy patterns that get worse as we get older, more ingrained, more difficult to break.

We scatter pieces of our identity and independence in the name of the very things love is not.

Love does not leave you empty.

Why is it that we are so willing — eager, desperate — to turn our backs on the undeniable, beautiful fact that we were created whole?

I was created whole.

Heartbreak is so incredibly painful it has made me wish that I was dead.

When you are in the grip of that feeling of devastation and emptiness there is only one person to turn to: yourself.

Love yourself with that same ferocity. Turn this passionate declaration *"I am willing to do anything in the world"* on yourself.

Be willing to do anything in the world for you.

Listen to lyrics of songs and deliberately change them.

I can't live if living is without me.

Keep doing that until you feel the grace and dignity that is true love.

Until you cannot see any other alternative but walking away from anyone who doesn't love you the way you deserve to be loved.

Until the person that you love does not need you, can easily live without you, is utterly complete already, but wants very much to stay.

Inner Circle

We were friends. Good friends. Until she came over to me at a party and accused me of horrible things.

I listened at first, then asked her to stop. But she wouldn't stop. That's when I realized she was deriving pleasure from the fact that she was hurting me.

I cried that night. Not over what she said. Over the disbelief of having witnessed my friend become somebody else. Someone I didn't know. A stranger. A foe.

She sent a long email late the next day. She explained that nothing of what she said had anything to do with me. She was going through things, she wrote, and inexplicably took it out on someone she knew would not counterattack. She apologized.

I forgave her. I tried to get things back to the way they were. But I could not.

The people you let in close, your inner circle, are those who support you, who want what's best for you. Not aggressors. Not people who enjoy your discomfort.

"Frenemy" is not a word.

It's entirely possible for a friend to disagree with me or tell me I am dead wrong. But this can, without exception, be delivered free of cruelty.

You teach people how to treat you, and I don't want to have to be wary of my friends. From my friends what I want is love.

Social Protocol

When I was 19, I spent a lot of time and effort trying to fit in.

Later in life I had to work hard at distinguishing what I actually liked versus what I did as a result of social pressure.

For example, it was tough for me to understand why I felt so depleted and lonely after a party. I learned later that despite being gregarious I was an introvert and spending so much time surrounded by others, even if they were friends, was draining me and leaving me with little time and energy to pursue things I loved.

I believe that part of the reason why it's so common to feel lost later in life is because our effort to follow social protocol has drowned out our inner voice.

Enabler

Imagine, if you will, that I'm always late for work. I'd like to fix this, but when the alarm goes off I hit the snooze button instead of getting up.

I hit the snooze button even if I have an important meeting. I hit the snooze button after I've been warned that I cannot continue to show up late. I hit the snooze button after I've hurt the people that I love by never being on time to what matters to them.

Being late is wreaking havoc on my life.

Now, imagine I live with someone who knows I need to fix this. My kind friend arranges my clothes by the bed. She leaves breakfast ready on the kitchen counter, finds and leaves my car keys somewhere visible.

My friend is "helping" by attempting to save me from the consequences of my own actions: this is what defines an enabler.

Instead of giving me space to correct my behavior, instead of recognizing my necessary sovereignty, she wants to rescue me, fix me, assist me — contributing to me not correcting anything.

It's incredibly difficult to stop enabling. It feels like, *well, if I can't do this, then who am I?* It feels like I can't do my favorite thing, which is to be helpful, useful.

It feels like you're leaving someone to drown.

But, it's the rescuing that does me in, because it makes it too easy for me to never learn how to save myself.

Over and Over:
Lose Yourself/Find Yourself

Let's say I meet a guy.

I like him a lot so I pretend to like what he likes.

I want decisions to be easy so I go along with whatever he wants to do.

Soon I can't tell if I like something or "we" like something.

This is how I delude myself into thinking I have lost myself.

The truth is I don't actually lose myself (although it feels that way). I am still here, making my voice heard in unsuspecting ways.

I get angry at small things, feel irritable and impatient.

I begin to speak up. It's a voice of dissent and this confuses the guy. All he has ever known is me agreeing with everything so I can't fault him for suddenly not recognizing me. I have never let him see me.

Speaking up feels good. It feels right. I do it in small ways first, and as my voice grows stronger I speak up in more meaningful ways.

I'm afraid, of course. Of losing his approval, of this guy deciding maybe we don't have that much in common and that he doesn't like me anymore.

139

But I've had enough of compromising myself and decide to push through this fear.

I'd rather not be liked by him than not be liked by me.

I don't want to go back to feeling lost, so empty and confused; not remembering what it's like to stand up for who I am.

And that's how you find yourself.

Shoes

Imagine that someone with the best of intentions gives you a pair of shoes.

You put them on and they are too tight.

Not only that. They are the wrong style for your uniquely shaped feet.

You take a few steps and your toes begin to hurt.

You decide not to say anything.

What if you offend the person who gave you the shoes?

What if they decide they don't like you anymore?

Have you ever worn uncomfortable shoes? Let me tell you. No matter how much you want them to fit, after a few hours you can no longer pretend.

Taking them off and wearing the right shoes will transform your life.

Your feet, rather than blistered, bleeding, eventually permanently damaged, will feel like they grew wings.

A pair of shoes right for you will take you to places you now can only dream of.

Even when you really want to, you cannot go through life pretending to be something you are not.

The earlier you change into the right pair of shoes the better.

Is It Time Yet?

You know that feeling of waking up in the morning with your heart full, *I don't want to eat or sleep or do anything other than be with him is it time yet is it time yet?*

I know that feels like love. And I'm not saying it isn't.

But it's not healthy love.

Healthy love is not codependent. It's never *"the two of us are one".*

And, what about *"We never fight! Not ever!"*? That's not healthy either.

If you don't fight, you never establish boundaries. The solidity of the relationship is not put to the test.

In healthy relationships you occasionally fight. You fight well and you fight fair. You don't say *"all"* or *"never"* or *"always".* You don't dredge up the past seventeen arguments. You are not intentionally hurtful — there are no low blows. You argue over the issue, rather than attack the person. You are specific. *"You hurt my feelings when you interrupted me"* rather than the dramatically sweeping *"You have no respect for who I am!"*

What about unconditional love? Unconditional love sounds deceptively romantic, but it's not healthy. Unconditional love equals no boundaries. Just like you need to treat each other with respect, you also need to respect yourself.

In healthy love, you are individuals, independent. There is no *"need".* You each have whole lives without the other: friends, interests, pursuits. This is not scary, because you trust. You trust yourself.

A healthy relationship is capable of evolution, because life is uncertain, because who you both are is in perpetual transformation, and because everything — everything — will change.

Your significant other will test your patience (sometimes a lot), will reveal where you need to grow, will inadvertently help you identify your boundaries.

You will be better for having him in your life.

He (or she) will be your accomplice — not your lifesaver, not your flotation device — in this magnificent, wild, erratic, inconstant, bewitching journey that is life.

Volunteer

The first time I ever got a job I volunteered for everything.

I did it in part because I suffer from excessive enthusiasm, but also because I am nosy and like being a part of things.

It didn't take long for me to feel resentful about my impossible workload.

Why didn't my company respect my time? Why did this organization say "it was the people who mattered" and no one did anything about the fact I worked evenings and weekends?

Why was the company taking advantage of my generosity?

I eventually came to realize two things:

The first was that this was not the company's fault, or my manager's fault. The person to blame was me. I dictate the rhythm of my life and no one can help me with that.

The second is that feeling trapped is a symptom of the presence of a double bind. Whatever is making me feel good is also making me feel bad.

Volunteering for everything ended up making me feel angry, but I couldn't stop because volunteering for everything also made me feel indispensable, and I didn't want to give that up.

We set the traps that catch us.

I'm 21 and Find It Difficult to Set Boundaries. How Do I Do Better?

I'm waaaay older than you are and also experience difficulty setting boundaries. This is because boundaries are hard to set. Also, they change constantly so require regular maintenance, upkeep and redesign.

But, boundaries are how I love myself.

The first thing I do is spend time with me. In this quiet space I answer two questions: what is my boundary? And, what about setting it is hard?

For example: I love my friends but in the current COVID-19 environment, I can't see them. It's not safe. My age does not matter. *"I love you but cannot hang out, and don't know when I will be able to"* is a brand new boundary.

I think it's hard because I worry my friends will feel I don't care about them. And because I don't know what the future looks like. I can't say *"I can't see you today but what about next week?"*

I soothe myself by talking things through with me. *Dushka, you can tell your friends "I sure wish I could see you, but this virus is terribly contagious and we need to be as safe as we can."*

Dushka, it's important that little by little you get comfortable with uncertainty. We don't know what the future looks like, but will manage it one day at a time.

This is how I set boundaries. Small step. Check in with myself. Small step. Soothe myself. Small step. Express my boundary. Small step. Learn to hold it.

Boundaries also tell me so much about other people. You are pushing on my boundary even though you know you could make someone sick, even kill them? You are arguing with me even though I'm trying to take care of my health? You've lost interest in our friendship because we can't "have a good time"?

I think this is really important information in my quest to take good care of myself.

I Want to Help

Do you know what I want?

I want to help.

I feel this compulsive desire to help inside me and I know it comes from a place of universal love. It comes from a place that's noble. It comes from a place that's open and casual and feels like a given.

But also it comes from a place of ego. Helping is a form of manipulation.

Helping grants me a role. A role is a shortcut: I don't need to figure myself out if I have a role. A role is an easy answer to most of my nagging existential questions. Helping provides significance, direction, purpose, meaning.

If you need me, I matter.

In the beginning, my offer to help might be almost insistent. *Let go. I can do this — it's easy. It's nothing. It makes sense. We are a team.*

Later I will look back and think it's like I forced you to take advantage of me.

As I help, and my role becomes defined, regular, a routine, you get used to this help. This is how it moves from that open and natural place inside me to a place that's tighter, more constricted, where it takes increasing amounts of effort.

You now expect me to do this thing that I do. You take it for granted. You take me for granted. I feel less generous, less willing, more put upon.

This makes me resentful as hell.

Resentment feels like I am angry at you, but really I'm angry at myself. I have not been clear with my boundaries. I have compromised myself. I have betrayed myself.

I did this. I did this to me.

As I try to pull out of this arrangement that has gotten out of hand, you go from surprise to indignance to feeling betrayed to feeling like I've changed to manipulating me. *"It was us — us against the world,"* you tell me. *"We said we were a team and now you've left me here to drown."*

I feel exhausted all the time.

To stop enabling I need to — well, I need to stop. I need to clean the slate and start over. I need to have the presence of mind to change the rules I designed. I need to get better at creating and enforcing boundaries.

I used to do this for you, and that was then and this is now and I'm not going to anymore. I have not been helping you. I have protected you from the consequences of your own actions. What I've done is incapacitate you. You are capable — have always been capable — of doing it for yourself.

My now grown-up boundaries have two painful requirements: I have to accept being misunderstood. I have to hold the discomfort of disappointing the very people I most want to impress.

But there is a much bigger trap, a more complicated knot to undo, which is the one I've tied to myself and my own identity.

If I am not helping you, what does this say about me? Where does this leave me? What is my purpose? If I define myself as "helpful", who am I if I walk away?

Tell me. How can anyone ever want to stay if they have not been ensnared by me being useful?

To stop enabling, I need to understand — not at an intellectual level, but in my heart — that I am worthy of being loved even when I'm not helping.

What this means is that to stop enabling I need to get to work on redefining myself.

Nice

Imagine you don't like pizza. The guy you are dating really likes it so you say you love pizza to make him like you.

You don't like pizza and end up eating pizza often rather than speaking up.

You risk ending up angry at him for always picking pizza.

Your anger builds up. You can't see it now but you are not angry at him. You are angry at yourself.

This is people-pleasing.

Now imagine you don't like pizza and all your friends like it. You say you don't like pizza, but you like spending time with them so decide that you can be flexible, that this time you can set your preferences aside to be accommodating.

That's being nice.

I understand how this can be a fine line but the first will make you feel used and resentful and diminished and the second will make you happy because you own where you stand and are being generous.

People-pleasing is not about making things easier for others but rather involves compromising who you are. It means trying to make everyone happy at your expense and realizing that despite your effort it cannot be done.

It's a losing battle to play against yourself.

It's sacrificing you to such an extent you lose track of who you are.

That's not nice. Nice begins by being nice to yourself.

Codependent/Interdependent

Codependent —

What you think of me defines me.

What others think of me takes up most of my time.

I am responsible for your feelings and can fix them.

I want you to like me.

I want you to approve of me and the choices that I make.

I will never say no or exercise any boundary.

What the heck is a boundary?

Do you need boundaries in the presence of true love?

My love is unconditional.

You will fix me and rescue me and save me.

I will fix you and rescue you and save you.

I hate being alone.

I can't really function on my own.

Interdependent —

I take responsibility for myself and for my feelings even when our lives are intertwined.

I feel safe enough to show you who I am.

I feel safe enough to say no, set and enforce boundaries.

I respect your boundaries.

We can hold the fact that boundaries are flexible.

I see you without getting me tangled up in what I see.

We can have different, even opposing opinions, and can remember events differently without feeling like we have to convince the other.

We enjoy time away from each other.

I like you and you like me.

I admire you and you admire me.

Your evolution, growth and transformation do not threaten or scare me.

This Is What You Get

The last time I was in a relationship we loved each other very much and were incompatible. We both tried for years to adjust, to change, to somehow make things work.

During that time I went to visit my mother and spent a weekend in her house. I didn't tell her very much but she saw me frazzled, frustrated, tired.

"Things are not going to change, you know."

"But, how can you say that?" I told her. *"Are people static? Do we not learn, get better?"*

"I am not saying people don't change. I am saying you two have been together long enough for you both to know that what you have is what you'll get. The question is — is this what you want? Is what you have right now the way you accept things will be for the rest of your life?"

She was right, so I will say it again.

It's not that things can't change. It's that for the most part, what you have right now is what you'll get. The question that only you can answer is — is this what you want?

Consequences

When I was in my early teens I dated a guy who drank — a lot. I believed not only that I could save him, but that it was my duty. I felt like leaving him would constitute an act of the deepest disloyalty.

Once, in despair, I attended an AA meeting to better learn how I could help him. I am going to tell you what I was told.

If you feel now the way I felt back then, this is going to hurt, and for that I am deeply sorry.

"Dushka — if you have ever done anything for him that in any way shields him from the consequences of his own actions, this is the definition of an enabler. Your presence enables him. You standing by his side enables him. You taking him back enables him. You looking the other way when he lies enables him. You recovering from him letting you down enables him.

"Do you see? This is a vicious cycle and you are a part of it, Dushka."

What did I say to this? What did I say when the counselor explained that I needed to stop being an enabler?

I said *"I can't".* I can't, because if I'm not helping, who am I? I can't because I don't turn my back on people I love.

I can't leave him to drown.

The counselor responded to this with a look. He didn't say the words but I understood.

The guy I was with was drinking — but the addict was me.

I think he saw this realization hit me because the next thing he said he said more gently.

"Do you love him?"

"Yes," I said.

"Then you need to leave him."

Is There a Time and Place for Codependency?

A relationship is defined as "codependent" when I hang on to the other to meet any need I should be meeting within myself.

This kind of relationship is unhealthy because it carries more than it should. I expend an unsustainable amount of energy keeping propped up something that should be able to hold itself up.

It's like swimming and drowning the person I love in an effort to remain afloat.

Here are some of the things someone in a codependent relationship would say:

I am not enough.

Without you, I wouldn't know what to do with my time.

I am either with you or waiting.

I would do anything to make you happy, even if it compromises me.

I don't know how to say no because it makes me feel you won't love me anymore.

If you don't approve of me or if you disagree with me I will lose you forever and I can't live without you.

158

I want to tell you what to do, tell you who you can be friends with and in general try to control you because I cannot survive without you. It's for these reasons that I am territorial, jealous, possessive and scared.

I am afraid to tell you the truth.

I feel responsible for your feelings.

And now, here is the trickiest, sneakiest symptom of a codependent relationship:

You read about it, recognize yourself and secretly think *"clearly, I am not codependent. It's just that I love madly, deeply, and others are selfish and don't know how to truly love".*

To make things even more complicated, pretty much every fairy tale, movie, song lyric and poem expresses codependency. This is why it's so hard to recognize just how unhealthy it truly is.

Constant Validation

If I need constant validation, this insatiable yearning betrays a pattern of people-pleasing and looking for approval that becomes my guiding principle.

This means that how others will react to my choices takes precedence over me listening to my own needs.

It means I will quickly adapt, shifting who I am to who I think others want to see.

It means I am hyper-intent on reading the behavior of others which implies I experience difficulty making decisions and take everything personally.

It means that what is familiar to me is a partner or a friend who is unreliable and who I have to chase. My relationships all have something in common: they are a roller coaster of emotions.

It means I feel stuck and like I don't have control over my life. This is because I truly don't. I have given away control in exchange for approval and love.

This is an extremely painful, absolutely exhausting way to live. Instead of grounded, secure, I feel tired, shifty, unlovable. I feel responsible for things I have no power over. I feel doomed.

To get unstuck, the only answer is to begin a practice that will change the way I live my life. There are no shortcuts. Believe me:

if I had an easy answer, I would give it to you.

This practice has to do with noticing: look, I'm doing it again. I am doing this for approval, instead of doing it because I really want to, or doing it for me.

I don't berate myself. I am doing this because this is what I know, but I will, one action at a time, one day at a time, rewire myself, right down to my soul. *This is not who I am. This is what I've learned, and I'm going to unlearn it.*

Unlearning this will change everything.

This practice has to do with abandoning the notion that I have to help or fix others, or make others happy. It has to do with freeing myself from the arduous, futile work of managing what others think or feel.

It has to do with beginning to create something for me. Space to be alone. A morning ritual where I get up and take deep breaths and write. Sacred time to listen to myself.

It has to do with learning to create boundaries. Creating a boundary is really hard because it runs counter to what was once my guiding principle. It means putting myself first over getting another person to love me. (Throughout this process I will lose people. I will also learn that the right people will stay.)

It has to do with observing every habit, every action, and committing to taking care of myself. To giving myself what I need. *You need to be validated, Dushka? You need to feel you are not alone? You need someone you can count on? I am right here.*

I am not implying we do not need others. I am not describing a practice of selfishness or isolation. Make no mistake: to me, connection is the meaning of life.

What I am saying is that I need something steady to stand on to give the best of myself to others: not someone desperate, grasping, needy, but someone certain, solid, strong.

He Is Treating Me Poorly

No matter what I write, you will break up with your boyfriend when you are good and ready, and that's OK.

What I want to say is that this is precisely how you learn to love yourself.

When you feel someone is treating you poorly and know you should not be the target of poor treatment.

When you feel you are walking on eggshells for someone and recognize you should not be living like that.

When you tell yourself *"I can't bring myself to do this"* and suddenly *"I just can't"* becomes *"I can't believe what I just did."*

You walk away and it hurts so much and instead of telling yourself *"my life is over"* you say *"I feel like crap right now but eventually I will heal, and this is how that healing begins."*

Then, slowly, you start to learn to set boundaries and stand up for yourself. You stand up for yourself and stop feeling like you have to betray yourself to keep people in your life.

Every single time you do that, you recover. You reclaim yourself.

You start walking away from the notion that you have to sacrifice yourself at the feet of the people that you love. You stop trying to control what another person does or feels. You stop needing another person's approval: what you need is to approve of yourself.

Everything, everything you need — to be treated well, to be loved for who you are, to be seen, to be appreciated, to be believed in — you have to start by giving to yourself.

I understand how deeply you feel you can't bring yourself to do what you know you need to. But you can, my friend. You most certainly can.

What if My Family Is Abusive?

One of the main ingredients of a happy life is the practice of boundaries.

Exercising them means exercising them. It doesn't matter how people react to them, and it doesn't matter who the people are.

Many times we allow our boundaries to be trampled on because the person who tramples on them is family. Because, *"family is everything".* Because *"blood is thicker than water."*

We are stuck in believing family automatically deserves a free pass.

An absence of boundaries is unhealthy, and particularly unhealthy within the dynamics of family.

This looks different inside of each family, but some examples of poor family boundaries are: abuse that is hard to identify because it's what you've always known, family members being extremely involved in matters that for you are private, the sense that you are responsible for everyone getting along, a parent insisting you be who they wanted to be, instead of who you actually are.

Keeping your family away is something only you can decide. Nobody needs to understand it, support it, or approve of it but you.

The decision might make you feel awful, because if you've never had clear boundaries they make you feel like you are being disloyal or failing someone important to you.

But, boundaries are key to your mental health.

Making a new life for yourself will help you heal. It will end a pattern that tends to continue across generations (abused people abuse people).

It will help teach you to listen to your own voice, to decide how you want your life to be, to show yourself that there is no reason why your upbringing has to be your destiny.

It helps to remember boundaries are never fixed. They shift, and pushing someone out of your life for the sake of your health does not have to be forever.

What Does Saying No Look Like?

I can and should say no if someone else wants to touch me and I don't want to be touched, or even if someone says something about my body that is not appropriate. If a stranger says, for example, *"You look hot in that dress,"* I can say *"Don't do that. It makes me uncomfortable."*

I can and should say no if someone is pushing on the way I think. If I do not (or do) believe in God and someone is imposing their beliefs on me, *"Don't force your beliefs on me"* would be the right thing to say.

I can and should say no if I need time alone and my friends are insisting I go out. My time and how I spend it is mine, and I need to protect it. I can say no, and don't need a reason. *"I can't join you this time but thank you so much for thinking of me."*

My things are mine. I can and should say no if someone is insisting I lend them my clothes or anything that belongs to me. Refusing to lend anything that is mine is my right.

I can and should say no if someone wants to talk about something I don't want to talk about. What if what I am hearing puts me in an awkward position? *"I would rather not discuss that, thank you."*

My body, my rules. My time, my rules. My energy, my rules. My things, my rules. If it's mine I get to decide.

This outline has to be clear but doesn't have to be combative, aggressive or threatening. It can be gentle, subtle and firm.

Sometimes, though, saying no is not enough. Sometimes the fact I said no makes the other person push harder. It's common for people to push on boundaries. We ourselves do it to others to get what we want.

"Whoa! I didn't mean to insult you when I said you looked hot. It was a compliment!"

"The fact you don't want to lend me your scarf is so selfish. Why do you only think of yourself?"

I need to learn to protect my boundaries. This can be calm, without being hesitant or feeble.

"Oh, come on! Come to the party! You need to learn how to have fun!"

"It certainly sounds like fun, but I really want to go home now. I will call you tomorrow so you can tell me about it!"

Saying no is not just OK. It is necessary.

But How Do I Learn to Say No?

To say no, it helps me to understand why I say yes (when I want to say no).

Here are my most common reasons:

Because I want you to think highly of me.

Because I want you to like me.

Because I don't want to fight.

Because I don't want to disappoint you.

Because I don't want to hurt you.

Because I don't want to feel like a bad friend.

Because I don't want to feel guilty.

Because I don't want to be difficult.

Once I identify the reason, I ask myself three questions:

If what I am afraid of actually happened, would it be such a terrible thing? (For example, I don't want to disappoint you but I also don't want to give you the impression that I am someone I am not — now that I thought it through I think it's healthier to disappoint you.)

Is this thing I am worried about really true? (For example, if you are my friend and I tell you I don't want to go out because I am trying to go to the gym instead, is this truly going to make you like me less, and if so, what does this say about our friendship?)

Should I be saying yes? (Maybe I don't feel like going to the movies but should I just go because it might be fun once I am there?)

This is how it becomes easier to say no — or, you know. Yes.

Why Does Everyone Keep Stealing Pieces of Me?

I am visiting my mom and she is sad because I'm leaving tomorrow.

I frequently feel like everyone wants a piece of me. Like I need to be in two places at once. Like everyone wants more — more time, more attention.

What this means is that I have to establish and fortify my boundaries. Get better at saying no. Hold firm.

But also I recognize that I am in a privileged place.

I figure that if everyone wants more of me rather than less, there must be something I am doing right.

And by me, I mean you.

What Decisions Should You Never Have to Justify?

I suffer from a nearly unbearable urge to justify myself.

People who are important to me often want me to do what they want and not what I want.

It has taken me many years to step into the fact that I make my own decisions (concerning my own life) and should not need to explain myself.

Some examples:

My outlines — where I end and someone else begins — are clear to me. I am not "we". I am just "me".

I work hard to not cast blame and to take responsibility for my own shit.

I can't "make you happy". I cannot "make you miserable".

I don't have what you need.

My body. It's mine. Sometimes I want to be touched (ok, most of the time) but sometimes I don't.

Saying "no" is hard for me (and getting oh so much easier as I get older). Don't push against it. Don't mess with it. Leave my "no" alone.

My privacy. I am pretty open about my computer, my phone and my things but I see no reason why anyone would go through them without my permission.

Protecting myself. If you deliberately hurt me, cause me pain or diminish me with your actions or with your words I will walk away, even if I love you.

Fighting fair is a requirement, and toxic people ("frenemies", people who deliver backhanded compliments, people who for reasons I cannot explain drain me or leave me confused and doubting myself) have no place in my life even if they are dear to me. Even if they are family.

I need time alone and I need silence. Noise affects me deeply. I will seek both of these things every day. This will often imply me sacrificing time with people that I love.

Resentment is a symptom that somewhere, somehow I have compromised myself.

I realize I'm not angry at you but at me, and I will use some of my quiet alone time to re-evaluate what happened so I can do better next time.

What Are Some Tips to Keep From Burning Out?

If I were to pick a single reason why people get burned out (and by "people" I mean me) it's the illusion that things will not function without me.

It's really hard to let this go because it would imply I am not indispensable.

I mean, ouch.

We burn ourselves out in order to preserve our ego.

To put it in other words, in the name of our ego we are willing to make ourselves sick, miserable and unhappy.

This is not a good bargain.

As such, the place to begin is to set my ego aside. Learn that the world does not stop spinning if I am not in it.

Things can get done well without my constant, active intervention.

This is painful but ultimately incredibly liberating.

Then, I need to learn how to set better boundaries. Leave the office during lunch. Take a stroll. No more working late into the night or working weekends. Because, whose fault is it if I say yes to everything? (In case you're wondering, mine. It's my fault.)

I try (mostly unsuccessfully) to take breaks from technology. Turn my phone off in the evenings. Power down on Saturdays or Sundays.

I find time to dedicate to anything I do that is creative. Paint. Write. Sculpt. Take a class to learn how to do something I've always been curious about. Activate new parts of my brain. (I really like ceramics so maybe this year I'll learn how to make my own bowls.)

Relax. Nap. Wander. Loiter. Take a bath. Read something that is not on a screen or device. (I actually do all of these things very well.)

Exercise. Activities with a cadence work particularly well: jogging, walking, swimming, yoga. I find my breath.

Eat well. My body does a whole lot better when I feed it nourishing, unprocessed, whole foods.

I sleep. This is very difficult.

I rediscover the joy and power of laughter. Laughter is a recovery balm so I actively look for people and things that make me laugh. (Fortunately I have a very simple sense of humor so this is not hard.)

When I can, I take a sabbatical (it doesn't have to be a long one). I take a solid break from everything and find a different, slower rhythm. I set my eyes on beautiful things.

I develop gratitude for all the things that used to irritate me (thank you so much, slow barista, for giving me the chance to catch my breath).

Then, maybe, integrate all of these things back into my real life. *Remember, Dushka. Nobody needs you, and that is the best part.*

What Have You Done to Avoid Ruining the Moment?

Many years ago I met a guy at a beach resort in Mexico, where I am from.

We started talking at the pool, later walked over to the beach, strolled along the water, had a late lunch of tacos and guacamole and sat down on towels to watch the sun go down.

As the sky turned orange and purple and pink I could tell he was thinking about leaning over to kiss me.

I didn't want to kiss him — I liked him but not like that — but I really didn't want to ruin such a beautiful moment.

What to do?

It turns out I didn't have to think about it very much at all. As he came closer, my body recoiled on its own.

He was angry. As if kissing me was his right. *"I can't believe you would ruin a sunset,"* he said.

His response was so disagreeable and such a contrast to how pleasant he had been earlier that he made me feel proud of my reaction instead of regretful.

If I don't feel like doing something I won't do it no matter what I might be doing to the moment.

If I ruin a moment, I know I can create many other beautiful ones.

Why Do People Push on Our Boundaries?

If a Friend Cuts You Out of Her Life, Would You Ever Reach Out?

Cutting someone out of your life is an aggressive, definitive move.

If a friend cuts me out of her life, what she is saying is she doesn't want me in it. Reaching out to her would go against her wishes.

It would be aggravating, disturbing, and, as such, the very definition of harassment.

When a Girl Asks for Space but Continues to Text, What Do I Do?

The last time I was in a similar predicament I realized that in my effort to try to figure out what to do, I was not being very fair to myself.

"Hey", I said. "I really respect your need for space. Just like you need space, I need clarity. I want to give you what you need, but I'm not clear on what that is. The fact that you ask for space, then continue to text or call me is something I find confusing. I don't know what I'm supposed to do, and that's an awful, frantic feeling.

"What I've decided is I need space too. This state of not knowing what to do is painful and I need time to sort myself out. How about I call you in a few weeks and we talk about where we are at then?"

Saying this was so hard. But I decided I deserved better than to put myself in a perpetually perplexing place.

Boundaries: A Moving Target

I spend my days testing and pushing people's boundaries. We all do. We don't know what they are because they vary per individual, moment by moment, with our own intention, and probably with the weather and other unspecified meteorological conditions.

I also test and push people's boundaries because I try to make my world more convenient for me. I suppose I'm often selfish, on the grounds that I'm human. We want what we want, and we negotiate to get it.

I am constantly weighing my own boundaries. It's extremely difficult. They are a moving target.

I believe in generosity. I will go out of my way to put others before myself. This makes me feel expansive and in control. A lot of my happiness resides in my ability to do things for others.

If anger creeps in, or resentment, I have overstepped. I have neglected myself, and that is a boundary I will defend and be unwilling to negotiate.

No one else can do this for me.

Boundaries Are Not About You

Boyfriend and I had just started living together and I really wanted to be the best possible girlfriend.

I was thinking about the inevitable discrepancy between what is most important to me and where I put my time.

From Monday to Friday, I spend roughly 3 hours a day with my significant other and 10 hours a day at work.

I resolved to make sure I had energy for him at the end of the day: to welcome him home with a hug and a smile; to talk about our day over a nice dinner sitting at the dining room table rather than in tired fragments mumbled during commercial breaks.

So I hear his keys rattle against the keyhole. I open the door wide and hug him and kiss him and welcome him home.

"Honey," he says *"could you let me put my stuff down and take my jacket off and give me a few minutes to catch my breath?"*

I immediately feel like he's not happy to see me.

I was telling a friend about this calamitous turn of events and he asks: *"Dushka, why are you taking this so personally?"*

Me: *Huh?*

Him: *Is it possible that Boyfriend has things going on before his arrival to your house? That he had a long day, work to get through, traffic to sit through? You are a total introvert. Surely you understand when someone else needs space?*

Me: *Oh.*

This "separation" between how another person reacts and you will improve your relationships, make you less self-centered, reduce unnecessary drama and forever set you free.

Money and Your Ex

Situation: when you were together, you told your ex you'd help pay for school. Now, you are no longer together and he's asking you for money. You are wondering if you should pay.

Someone is asking you something related to your money. The money belongs to you, so you get to decide what to do with it.

If you decide to help him pay for the class, for whatever reason, even for no reason, that is your call to make.

If you decide that you once wanted to but don't want to anymore, that is also up to you.

If you don't want to pay for his class anymore — which would be understandable, since the circumstances have changed since you initially offered — what you need to do is say no.

No.

You don't need to explain your no. You don't need to apologize for it.

You do need to learn to get comfortable with the fact you might disappoint him. He might feel let down. He might even push and tell you you're going back on a promise.

This is what defines a boundary: it can change, it often feels awful and almost like a betrayal, and in the end what you are left with is your power over your person and what belongs to you.

A boundary is how you love yourself, how you stand up for yourself, and how you show others where your limits are.

One more thing: how someone reacts to a boundary you set reveals a lot about that person. If someone disrespects your boundary, they are disrespecting you.

Does No Mean Yes?

When I was growing up in Mexico men having sex were displaying virility and prowess and women having sex were sluts.

This put women in a position where they needed to pretend they didn't want sex and played coy and said no when they really wanted to say yes.

This put men in a position to assume no could mean yes if they pushed.

I don't mean to imply that this is women's fault or men's fault.

I mean to imply this is a vicious circle that muddles communication and makes consent something you have to interpret.

This is fertile ground for sexual assault.

Pop culture perpetuates this. The woman says no. The man pushes. The woman succumbs. We sigh.

Consider the first time Han Solo kisses Princess Leia.

She clearly, aggressively pushes him away. She says no. She says no again. She shakes her head.

He kisses her.

We think it's romantic.

No wonder we are confused.

What if we remove the game playing?

Women would have to admit to liking sex as much as men like sex (and I do).

Then, the initiator would say something along the lines of *"I'd like to kiss you. Is that OK?"*

If I said no that would mean he would understand, take a step back and not kiss me.

I could not afford to take this risk if I really did want him to kiss me, so I'd say yes.

We would live in a world where no would mean no, and yes would mean yes.

If anyone thinks this is in any way less romantic let me tell you there is nothing as conducive to good sex as clear communication.

I Don't Want My In-Laws in the Delivery Room. What Do I Do?

This is excellent.

You are about to become a mom. Your baby will need you to protect her and keep her safe. To do this, you will need to hone your boundary-setting skills.

What an important place to start.

This baby is growing in (and will come out of) your body. This means you're the boss. You get to decide who's invited to be in the delivery room.

I understand this can be a difficult boundary to lay down and enforce, but it's just the beginning of a life-long discipline: lovingly showing the world, including your husband's parents, what your sacred limits are: in your life, in your home and with your baby.

My hope is that you are able to recruit your husband in this effort, that he can understand this is a new life, and that a baby changes everything.

How Can Those Who Do Nothing for Others Be Well-Liked?

If someone likes me, they have a favorable feeling towards me, appreciate me and my company, find me agreeable.

People like me for who I am, not for what I can do for them.

If someone "likes" me because I do them a favor, that's not "like". That's convenience. Their feelings for me will change if I stop doing things for them, and that's not really the kind of arrangement I'd want to make with anyone.

If I believe the only way to be liked is to do things for others, this means I am likely to compromise my boundaries. It means I will say "yes" when I want to say "no", that I will sacrifice what I want to make room for what another wants, often without them even knowing.

The common thread of my relationships will be resentment, feeling needy and used.

Boundaries — such as saying no or expressing what I want — are a wonderful filter. They annoy, irritate and ultimately lose the interest of those who want us for what we can do — but, you know who stays? The ones who love us for who we are.

How Do You Attract a Good Partner?

For many years I was convinced that if a man did not experience jealousy he was not that into me. If he told me he didn't want me to have guy friends, possessively put his arm around me in public places, and acted a little bit crazy if he suspected someone was flirting with me, I felt loved and wanted and protected.

Then I wondered why all the men I dated were so dominating, so irrational, and so controlling. My god. Where were all the good men?

During that same time, if I dated a guy who was not possessive, who considered me having guy friends a non-issue, and who completely trusted me I interpreted this as a dismaying absence of interest.

It wasn't that I wasn't attracting good partners. It's that in a sort of trick of subconscious camouflage, I did not know how to recognize them.

I regret to inform you there is no short-cut or magic potion or spell or law that you are failing to understand or get right.

To attract good partners, you have to develop an awareness of your own patterns. You have to get to know yourself. You have to be the one who saves you.

You have to love who you are enough to only want what's best for her.

Will Handshakes and Touch Go Extinct Due to the Pandemic?

Originally, a handshake was a way to say *"I do not intend to hurt you."* Look, I am showing you my hand so you can see I am unarmed.

Now, if I shake your hand, I am saying *"I have no way to know if I am sick with something that could kill you or kill someone you love."*

Touch, hugs, kisses and high fives have different implications, as they can threaten not only the health of the people I come into contact with, but the people they love.

This moves me beyond consent. It wouldn't matter to me if you were OK with being hugged. It would not be something I would want to do.

Now, staying away and refraining from contact is a way to say *"I would not want to hurt you."*

I wouldn't say greetings that involve touch are extinct. But I would guess we will evolve into something different, like a bow, hands coming together in front of the heart, or eye contact and a nod.

Not because the world has changed, but because we have.

I Am 16. Can My Mother Control My Hairstyle?

If you are 16, in many countries you are considered underage.

Not always, but typically, your parents are fully responsible for you and take care of you. They also finance your life: you live under their roof, and if you get anything — from sneakers to an education — it's with their money.

That being said, you are your own sovereign person, and at 16 it's important to learn to establish boundaries.

So. State your case. Not in the form of a tantrum, a demand or an attitude that is sullen or ungracious or indignant. State your case like someone who deserves to be treated like an adult.

"Mom. I understand I am and will probably always be your baby. But over the years, I've become more my own person. I want to do something to my hair and I want to be heard. I want us to reach common ground. Because, this is not just about my hair. This is about working together as I grow up and fully claim the person you are almost done raising."

Then, you super patiently, truly, with an open heart, listen to her. You talk it out. My hope is that at the end of the conversation you will feel more self-possessed, and she will feel more admiring.

Maybe she holds the mirror up while you shave the side of your head.

Maybe she looks at you, closes her eyes and runs her hand gently over the soft stubble.

Maybe this is the point where you pave the way for a healthy relationship with someone who probably, if you are lucky, loves you with ferocity and as such is sometimes clumsy and at a loss about what to do with you.

It's your job to help her navigate who you are becoming.

Why Is She Hurting Me on Purpose?

One of the lessons I have had to learn over and over again is that I cannot change other people.

I cannot change other people.

Whenever someone does something that in any way makes me uncomfortable or unhappy my default is to wonder how to change them, then wonder why they won't change.

This is a huge expenditure of energy.

How? How? How?

Why? Why? Why?

Finally, I come to my senses and realize that the way out is me.

I am really sorry she (whoever she is) is hurting you on purpose.

We cannot change other people. We can only change ourselves.

As such, the question becomes *"Why do I allow in my life someone who is hurting me on purpose?"*

Am I Wrong to Need Time Alone?

I need a lot of time alone.

Through the years, I have learned that *"I need time alone"* is what I say, but that is not what others hear.

What they hear is:

Wanting time alone means you don't want to be with me.

Wanting time alone means your feelings for me are not strong enough.

Wanting time alone means you don't love me.

Wanting time alone means I am not your priority.

What this takes is communication, patience, education.

I try something like this:

"Maybe you are angry or hurt because you feel me needing time alone means I am not interested enough in you. Actually, it is not related to you. I had a long day and don't feel like talking."

This kind of conversation helps people understand each other better.

It helps people suffer less.

Because, think about it. She is not experiencing you being tired — she is experiencing you not caring about her.

Ultimately, if she needs a lot of your presence and you need a lot of time alone you might not be compatible — but before getting all the way to a conclusion of incompatibility, there is space. Space to work with.

What I want to say more than anything is she is not wrong in wanting more time with you, and you are not wrong in wanting time alone.

The real questions are — can you be patient with each other? Can you meet in a place that works for you both?

Can this effort open her up to not taking things personally — a lesson that will improve every part of her life?

Can it open you up to being better about how you communicate — a lesson that will improve every part of your life?

At its best, this is what love does. It changes us in a way that makes our whole life better.

Why Do We Choose People Who Don't Choose Us?

When I was little — maybe 11 — I wanted to be friends with a girl who never seemed particularly interested in being my friend.

At my (inexplicable) insistence we spent a lot of time together but the effort I put into the relationship was definitely one-sided.

One afternoon at her house I woke up to the fact that she always treated me with a bit of disinterest, even disdain.

I told her it was time for me to go home and never called her again. She never called me either.

Very shortly after I started hanging out with a girl who seemed happy to hang out with me. The friendship was effortless and natural. We remain in contact to this day, decades later.

In your question I believe you are referring to a romantic pursuit, and in my experience above I am referring to a relationship between two friends. I think what I learned still applies.

Trying to force a relationship of any nature with someone who exhibits reluctance or a lack of enthusiasm for me is likely to set the tone for how the entire relationship is going to be.

Lukewarm, disinterested, leaving me with the feeling that I somehow would never be enough.

I can't help but feel I deserve better than that.

If instead I invest time and effort in relationships with people who are just as enthusiastic about me as I am about them, I experience every day what it's like to be loved for who I already am.

So, I don't know exactly why I am sometimes interested in someone who is not interested in me — but I do know that when I feel this interest I have a choice.

I can ask myself what it is that I want: to be loved instantly and enthusiastically, or to struggle forever to attempt to show the other I am worthy of their love.

Why Do My Parents Act Exhausted When I Show Affection?

I am going to tell you something that is extremely difficult and extremely painful to understand but once you do it will set you free forever, and not just from what you are feeling now.

How people behave is related to their own experiences, their own history and how they feel about themselves.

Asking why someone acts a certain way after we do something assumes their actions reveal something about us, when instead they have nothing to do with us.

What this means is that you cannot measure anything about you by the way someone else behaves.

This would be the same as going to a library and determining what's in your book by reading snippets of the books everyone else is holding.

What this also means is that the affection you show is just right.

You are just right.

I know you won't believe me right now, but maybe some day you will.

Why Did the Guy I Rejected Stop Texting Me? Doesn't He Love Me?

This is a prime example of what is known as "a toxic belief".

If I say no to a guy and he continues to pursue me, this does not mean he loves me. It does not mean he is super interested.

What it means is he feels that what he wants takes precedence over the right I have over myself.

Do you see?

He sees me as an object, not a person.

If I believe the guy who loves me is the guy who overrides my boundaries, then the guys I let in are the ones who don't ever listen to what I say I want regarding myself.

My belief ensures the people I let close to me are the ones most likely to hurt me.

How Do I Recover From Losing a Friend for Setting a Boundary?

The scariest thing about setting boundaries — and the reason why sometimes I am not assertive enough — is that they might cost me my relationships.

But, someone willing to cross my boundaries is saying *"I am willing to get what I need at the cost of what you need."*

They are saying *"Your discomfort or you overextending yourself is OK if I benefit from it."*

Maybe I needed better relationships.

And that's how I get over losing someone.

Going Nowhere

My friend Patrick (not his real name) was married for many years to a woman he loved. His divorce devastated him. He knows he is not ready for a relationship but realizes too he doesn't want to live in isolation.

He dates women and clearly states he appreciates the company but is not looking for a relationship. *"I will be happy to see you"* he says. *"But also I do not want to get involved. If I spend time with you it's because I appreciate you, but I don't want a girlfriend or a wife or a significant other. I want to make clear this is going nowhere."*

Because what he is used to is being a husband, he very quickly gets comfortable with the person he is seeing. They get into an easy cadence that *feels* like a relationship.

They call each other, they go to the supermarket on weekends, they watch a movie at his apartment and have sex and wake up the next day and have breakfast.

After a week or two or six, the woman will say something like *"Where is this going?"* or *"My parents are coming into town and I wonder if you'd like to meet them"* or *"I love you."*

My friend is perplexed.

"But, I told you. I told you from the beginning, and reminded you along the way, that I am not looking for a relationship. I don't want a relationship, although I appreciate the company and like hanging out with you.

"I felt like I made that clear."

Sometimes the woman leaves but often she stays — or comes back. A slightly different version of the same incident happens a few weeks later. *"Hey — I'd love it if you'd meet my friends"* or *"I don't understand what we are doing"* or again *"I love you."*

The truth is that when we clearly state what we want that is no guarantee the other person can hear us.

We hear what we want to hear, or we hear what he said and think we can change it. Because, it will be different with me.

This is how we break our own heart.

If I meet a guy I like and he tells me he is not looking for a relationship, and a relationship with him is what I happen to want, it doesn't matter if he wants to hear my voice or if he looks at me with love in his eyes or if the sex is amazing.

If he says he is not ready for a relationship, I do my best to listen.

What Do Boundaries Sound Like?

What Are Good Reasons to Turn Somebody Down?

You are the master of the universe when the universe is you.

You decide it all: who to surround yourself with, who to frequent, who can touch you, how, where and when.

If you don't want to spend time with someone, if someone wants something you don't want, you don't need any reason.

"I am sorry, but I don't feel the same way" already holds everything you need.

What Do You Say to Someone Who Tries to Be Helpful but Isn't?

Whenever I'm with friends and we're eating and I come across something delicious, I have an urge to get everyone to try it.

Things go something like this:

"It's amazing. Have a taste".

"Nah, thank you."

This leaves me with the sensation that I'm selfishly experiencing something wondrous. They really should just try it.

"You really should just try it."

"No, thank you".

We chat and I continue to munch and notice I'm about to finish my meal. They will miss out forever.

"Hey. You're sure you don't want to try it?"

"Dushka! Gawd! Yes! I'm sure!"

A few weekends ago I was spending time with my niece and nephew. We all went to a restaurant for brunch and I got something I knew they'd love.

"Guys, guys! Who wants to try this delicious thing!?"

"No, thank you!"

"But, it's amazing. You'll love it."

"No, thank you!"

"Guys! You don't understand what you are missing! I just know that you —"

My seven year old nephew stands up, both arms in the air.

"AUNTIE DUSHKA STOP WE DON'T WANT TO TRY IT LEAVE US ALONE!"

So, yeah. That's what you say to them.

Stay or I'll Fire You

One day, many years ago, a woman who worked for me came into my office crying.

"The client just told me that if I go on vacation they will pull the account," she said. *"This vacation is so important to my family. We will all be there — three generations — to celebrate my mother's 80th birthday."*

The client she was speaking of was our largest, in an agency I was running.

"As your boss," I said, *"I'm going to ask that you not go on vacation. Now, as a person who cares about you beyond the walls of this office, I'm going to suggest you put your foot down and hold your boundaries. What measures are you taking to ensure that your absence does not affect his business? Talk to him about that. If you need me, I will be right here, but I suspect you will feel much better if you grant this to yourself."*

On their next call, here is what my friend said. *"I know you think I am vital to your business and I know that me leaving on vacation at this important time makes you nervous. But, I don't service your business on my own. I have a team, and I trust them, and you will have everything you need. If knowing this you feel the need to fire us anyway, it saddens me, but I cannot cancel this vacation to accommodate your event."*

He did not fire us.

Is Yelling at Someone a Boundary?

Setting boundaries is gentle, kind and firm.

"I love you and am going to spend Sunday by myself. I've had a long week and really need to recharge."

Boundaries don't ever have to be violent or severe. They are instead full of compassion.

"I have been feeling a bit anxious and scattered. I'm going to sort myself out and will call you in a few days."

Boundaries are pure love — the way you respect yourself but also the way you put yourself in the best possible position to grant others the best of you. Not you, tired. Not you, over-extended. Not you, resentful.

"I don't really feel like talking about my family today but there are so many other things we can talk about!"

Boundaries are not aggressive, mean, or selfish. Boundaries are not greedy or even self-indulgent. They are instead healthy, robust and full of life.

I Suck at Setting Boundaries

I tell myself I totally suck at setting boundaries and then I realize that's no way to talk to someone I love.

It's not that I suck. It's that it used to be OK for me to say yes to that, and now it's not.

I was fine with jumping on any chance to spend time with you, and now I would really appreciate it if you gave me a bit of notice.

I loved spending entire weekends with you and now I don't love you any less but need some time to myself.

I've learned that the thing to do is take a baby step and check in with me. Baby step, check. Baby step, check.

To communicate as clearly as I can. *"I know I've always said yes to this and that this might be really confusing, but what I used to say yes to doesn't feel comfortable anymore."*

And to be understanding that it's not that I'm too soft or too rigid. It's that I'm doing the best I can.

I'm pretty sure you are too.

Is "I Don't Like That Tone" a Boundary?

A boundary points at your own behavior.

Pointed at another person's behavior, it's an attempt to control.

"I don't like the tone of voice you are using with me" is a sentiment, but the action attached to it is unclear and as such not pointing at either you or me. For this reason it's not quite a boundary.

"I understand you feel strongly about this, but the tone you are using makes me shut down and if it continues I am going to have to resume this conversation at another time" points at me: boundary.

What Are Some Examples of Professional Boundaries?

After 7:00 pm I don't look at email.

I don't work on Saturdays but am happy to work on this on Sunday.

In order to deliver my work on time, here is what I need from you.

I am happy to schedule a call, just know I am not comfortable turning on the video camera.

I cannot travel until the risk of contracting the virus is brought under control.

Were You Born Knowing How to Set Boundaries?

Nobody is born knowing how to set boundaries.

As babies we depended on others to remain alive. Getting others to like us and approve of us is related to survival and runs contrary to learning how to assert our sovereignty.

As we get older, the absence of boundaries means bitterness, disrespect and resentment. It means the erasing of our outlines. We begin to disappear.

Clear boundaries mean clarity on where others end and I begin. They mean healthy relationships. Boundaries are how we love and stand up for ourselves but also how we give to others the best of us: the part that feels safe and happy rather than overextended.

Boundaries are a practice, not something you learn one time and then "get right".

It's normal for others to not like our boundaries, in particular when boundary setting changes the rules of the existing dynamic. For this reason we don't just need to set them, but also defend them.

Some boundaries are set from the very beginning of a relationship (*"if you are going to be late, please just let me know")* and some come up when something hurts us or makes us uncomfortable *("I understand you are angry but please don't slam the door").*

Many, many times boundaries come up as we go, so we are always new at setting them. Nobody is a boundary expert. Everyone is fumbling along.

Here are a few examples of what boundaries might look like:

No.

You making a joke at my expense hurts my feelings.

It's OK for us to disagree but you can't force me to think like you do.

Your party sounds so fun! I am sorry I cannot make it.

I just broke up with my boyfriend and I'm not ready to talk about it.

Please don't touch me like that.

If anything in a relationship makes you feel pushed, invaded, resentful, observe it. What do you need? What would make you feel more comfortable? Your answer is your boundary. It belongs to you, so you do not need to explain or justify it.

Finally, boundaries express your limits rather than control another. *"I want you to stop seeing other people"* is control, not a boundary. A boundary is *"I am monogamous and not interested in an open relationship."*

How Do I Remain Friends
With My Ex?

Here are the steps I follow:

First, I take some time to determine what I really, truly want. Do I really want his friendship, or am I having issues with the transition, with letting him go? This is important for me to internally identify because what contributes to making a mess of things is saying one thing and wanting another.

Then, I sit down with him and clearly spell out what I want. *"This relationship did not work out, but we worked out. I love you and I want you in my life and I want your friendship and what this means is that I'm willing to work through the pain and the awkward parts. I want to confirm you feel the same way. This means we will have to communicate and work together."*

If he agrees, then all the steps from here on out are decided by both of us. For example —

Let's take a couple of weeks from the break up to the first call, just so that we begin a friendship with a clean slate.

No sex or sexual activity (with each other). We're friends and the plan is to not mess things up.

If one of us starts dating we let each other know. If one of us feels like we are starting another serious relationship we let the other know.

When we start seeing someone else we make sure that person is comfortable with our friendship. This might mean introducing each other. We make a true, real effort to make the other person feel safe, because they are.

That's it. Things come up, and you navigate them by talking and figuring things out. For example *"I am hurting right now — I think I need time to process but let's talk once a week until I come out of this."*

Remaining friends with significant others has been for many years one of the most enriching, most rewarding, most loving parts of my life.

What Do You Say to Someone Who Keeps Hurting You?

Goodbye.

Should There Be Boundaries In Unconditional Love?

Just for the purposes of illustrating what a boundary does to a relationship, I will pick a simple example.

Let's say that I am dating a guy and I don't like it when he calls me while I'm working. A call is too jarring, too invasive, and it invariably comes when I'm in a meeting or on another call.

But, I really want to hear from him.

So every time he calls, I say nothing.

I feel irritated. I feel imposed upon. At first the excitement of hearing from him overrides this, but little by little my irritation grows.

It's impossible to feel this way — ruffled, unsettled — and not see friction seep into our conversations.

Pretty soon my tone when he calls is short, terse. I feel distracted and torn and like I need to be in two places at once.

I am afraid to ask him not to call me. What if he stops calling me? But his calls are disrupting my work.

One day I gather my courage.

"I love hearing from you," I say. *"But, taking your calls when I'm at work is hard for me. I wonder if you can text me instead."*

If he keeps calling, I stop picking up. When he calls, I let it go to voice mail, then text him. *"I saw that you called. I can't talk right now but am looking forward to calling you tonight."* This is me holding my boundary.

If he insists on calling even after I've spoken to him and explained things to him and held my boundary, I have to wonder what other boundaries he will push on. Disrespecting boundaries is a red flag.

"Unconditional love" is not romantic. It's unhealthy.

If he says something like *"yes of course! No problem!"* and switches from a call to texting me, he respects my boundaries and obliterates many issues that had the potential to fester: I feel free. I don't feel terse. I don't feel irritated. There is no friction.

This is the best thing I could have done for this nascent relationship.

What Are Three Things You Recommend to Me?

A stranger contacts me to say he read something I wrote and wants to feature it on his site. I reply that with proper attribution he's free to use it.

He asks if we can discuss.

I am hesitant to, because if he wants to feature my article and I've said yes, what else is there to talk about?

But I push through my hesitation because my writing matters to me.

The guy wants me to register on his new question and answer site to feature my article. I tell him I don't want to.

He tries to persuade me. I say no. He tries again.

"But why?" he says. *"Why won't you just register? It will take two minutes."*

I could say *"Because my time is my life, and I have to be diligent about how I use it. Because I always want to help, but helping you infringes on me helping myself. Because I've learned that it's my time, my rules. Because I've said no and you pushing me past that is entirely my fault for putting myself in this situation."*

Instead I say *"I don't need to answer that, but thank you for your interest in my writing."*

It's no longer interesting to me to be all things to all people. I don't feel the need to explain myself. I'm increasingly OK with disappointing others.

These are three things I highly recommend.

How Do You Avoid Answering a Personal Question?

I say *"that question is personal and I don't want to answer it."*

Is Ignoring Someone a Healthy Way of Setting a Boundary?

Deliberately ignoring someone is a form of aggression. It's callous and inconsiderate. It means I don't see you or acknowledge you. It makes you feel like you don't matter, or worse, like you don't exist. It's a form of emotional abuse.

Being ignored is difficult to recover from and often leads to the end of the relationship.

Setting a personal boundary would be more like *"I am processing a lot right now. I'm going to take some time to myself and will call you in a couple of weeks."*

What Is an Example of Setting Boundaries?

Are you protecting yourself? Respecting your own limits and clearly identifying what you are comfortable with?

Or is what you are requesting attempting to limit or control someone else?

Healthy boundary: *My family is important to me and I regularly spend time with them.*

Not a boundary: *You spend too much time talking to your sister and I don't think you should do that anymore.*

Here are a few examples of healthy boundaries, because they are related to you: your needs, your time, your body.

I want to furiously make out with you but am not ready to have sex.

I know you mean to be funny when you tease me but it hurts my feelings.

When you raise your voice at me I feel diminished and threatened.

I need time alone. It doesn't mean I don't want to be with you.

If you want to post a photo of us on social media I would like to see it before you do so to make sure I am comfortable making it public.

I am a private person. I love you but am not comfortable with you having my passwords or looking at my phone.

I am a committed, monogamous person but am not interested in marriage.

I want to share my life with you but don't want to have children.

Boundaries are not static. They change and and evolve, just like you.

Making out was awesome and now I'm definitely ready for sex.

How Do I Commit to a Relationship Without Losing My Freedom?

Start by defining what "commit" means to you. Forget about what it means to others. How do you envision it? What about this word makes you feel devoted rather than bound, willing rather than obligated?

Then, define what "freedom" means to you. Forget what it means to others. What do you want? What makes you feel trapped, stuck, cornered, unfree?

Once you are clear on those things, communicate your boundaries. An example might be *"I am committed to you, but I don't want to live with you. I like my own space and as such prefer to live alone."*

Or, it might be *"I am very committed to you, but I want an open relationship where we can see other people."*

Or, *"I want to marry you, live with you, not see other people, have a family with you, but I feel trapped when another person constantly tells me what to do or tries to control me."*

Different people are comfortable and happy with different things, and to "commit to a relationship without losing your freedom", you have to define it, and find people who define it similarly.

Being Touched Makes Me Panic and My Girlfriend Ignores This

I am so sorry this is happening to you. It sounds incredibly distressing and painful.

You needing to be warned before being touched is your boundary. It's your body — so you have the inalienable right to determine the rules of if, how and when you are touched.

It doesn't matter what anyone thinks.

The people you let close to you need to respect your boundaries. You don't ever need to explain or justify yourself.

What you can't do is change another person. You can't have any expectation of how your girlfriend is going to behave.

All you can do is say something like *"You need to warn me before touching me. I am sorry to say this is my boundary, and therefore not negotiable. If you can't respect it, I cannot be with you."*

I know this might feel really scary but you (and everyone) deserves to have people around you that respect what you are clearly stating are your personal limits.

Give yourself that. Give yourself an important first step in your own health: the ability to articulate and hold your boundaries.

Holiday Season Boundaries

Thank you so much for your interest but I don't want to discuss the status of my relationship/my career/my wildly interesting yet intensely personal sexual exploits.

Thank you so much for making my favorite dish. I'm trying to cut down on the amount of food I'm eating, but it sure looks delicious.

I'd love to have you over for drinks but you can't spend the night at my place this year.

I adore your kids but the party I am throwing tonight is adults only.

(Or, conversely — *I would love to come over but if I can't bring my kids I'm going to have to pass.*)

I'm not drinking tonight. Do you have sparkling water? (If you don't want to drink, my god. You don't need to explain or justify this decision.)

Does Forgiving Someone Mean You Have to Trust Them?

Have you ever gotten food poisoning?

You like shrimp and eat one and get horribly sick. You spend a few days feeling like you might die. Slowly, you recover.

The next time you see shrimp you can't. You just can't. Stay away from me.

This imperative — stay away — does not go through my heart. I don't hate shrimp. I don't feel resentful towards shrimp. I don't harbor ill-will towards it.

It's not intellectual either. I am not rationalizing or thinking. I'm not even using words. Just recoiling.

There are people in my life (fortunately, very few) that have hurt me that I have completely forgiven. I feel no trace of a grudge. But my system has identified them as poison, and as such I will keep them away from me.

The Difference Between Boundaries and Control

How Can You Know if You're in an Unhealthy Relationship?

I look at two things.

Boundaries and control.

Boundaries: when I am not sure where I end and the other begins.

One consequence of blurry outlines is the tendency to hold another responsible for what I am responsible for.

Here is what poor boundaries might look like:

We are one.

You are my other half.

We do everything together.

I can't live without you.

My purpose is you.

You are the only thing that interests me.

My life revolves around you.

You make me happy.

You make me whole.

(Or, conversely) *You are destroying me.*

Control: when I attempt to dominate another.

Here is what that looks like:

You need to be loyal and love me unconditionally.

You are too close to your family.

You can't have friends.

I don't trust you but you can earn my trust with impeccable behavior.

I need to keep an eye on you and spy on you and look through your things.

You can't wear that/eat that/do that.

I will criticize you to help make you better.

I will keep this relationship strong by making you doubt yourself and your abilities so you don't leave me.

I love you more than you love me and am keeping score.

A healthy relationship makes me a better person — not because I am imposing my definition of what that means on another, but because it inspires me to be better and as such I work on myself.

Has Anyone Ever Wanted to Control You?

I grew up in a conservative country, at a conservative time, with a particularly conservative dad.

He loved me and was overprotective and felt that if he could control everything — where I went, who I talked to, what time I got home — he could keep me safe.

He used to measure my skirts with a measuring tape before letting me leave the house.

Later, whenever I met a man who wanted to control me, it felt so natural. I felt tethered, protected.

This is what I knew love to be.

It's very difficult to unprogram how you have learned to define love: it's like your concept of it is formed, then gets tangled up in the delicate double helix of your DNA strands.

Now, whenever someone expresses a desire to possess or control me and my brain lights up like a Christmas tree, another more experienced part of my brain speaks to me softly.

"No, Dushka. I know this feels good, but this is not healthy."

To answer your question, yes, I have been in a relationship with someone who wants to control me. It feels like sunshine, and how I handle it is I walk away. It's really hard.

What Are the Signs You're Stuck in the Past?

If I wanted to know if I was stuck in the past, I'd check for the presence of any of these signs:

Low self-esteem: many of the ingredients of low self-esteem, such as a critical inner voice, come from our past and whatever or whoever programmed that voice inside us. In a sense, a healthy self-esteem comes from overcoming the parts of our past that made us second guess if we were good enough.

Bitterness: living with something that left an acrid aftertaste in my heart. It's hostile and harsh and the opposite of contentment and comes from the way I processed an experience.

Resentment: a sign that I was not clear when I set my boundaries, or that I didn't set them at all, thereby compromising myself.

Comparison: the happier I am with myself and the decisions that I make the less it occurs to me to use other people as a measure of how I'm doing. If I begin to compare myself to others this might indicate there is something I am stuck on.

Blame: blame is completely disempowering. It's the sense that someone else was responsible. If I can't change others, how can I address anything I was not responsible for?

Fear of change: everyone fears change but living in the present comes with a sense that I only need to manage the present moment as it presents itself.

Wanting revenge: this is one of the clearest signs I am living in the past. Instead of focusing on me, my own evolution and well being, I focus on what I can do to hurt somebody else.

It's extremely difficult to summon gratitude towards something that makes me bitter, but little by little I can turn something acrid, acid, painful, into something that grants me something priceless.

Which is to say, the antidote to all these feelings is a practice of gratitude.

Should I Forgive My Partner After He Beat Me and Then Apologized?

Of course you should forgive him.

This means that first you leave him, and then once you have gotten far away from him you work at wishing him no ill will.

Forgiving does not mean the person occupies the same place (or any place) in your life; nor does it imply that you carry on as if what you describe never happened.

You can forgive someone and resolve never to see them again. You don't distance yourself out of anger or spite but out of respect for yourself; out of a healthy need to set new boundaries.

Forgiving someone is not a gift to the person who hurt you but rather a gift to yourself.

The goal of forgiveness is freedom from resentment, bitterness, anger or hatred.

Harboring these feelings cannot hurt another person but can cause you and those around you great harm.

You deserve a life free of violence.

What Is Something Movies Always Get Wrong?

A man tells a woman he wants her.

The woman shakes her head no.

The man takes this "no" as "try harder."

The man begins a series of grand gestures, after which the woman collapses into his arms.

People. After "no", insistence is harassment.

If Everyone Is Manipulating, Is Anyone Manipulating?

If you have ever tried managing or handling another person, you have (or have tried) to manipulate them.

This refers to anything you do to get what you want: flattery, threats, charm, lies, words, twisting logic, the artistic use of words to form an elaborate argument that tilts in your favor.

Look. Look at how much sense it makes for you to do what I want.

Parents, lovers and children are masters of manipulation, bribery and blackmail.

Do you want to grow big and strong like your brother? Finish what's on your plate.

No more video games until you finish your homework.

Call me when you get there or I will be worried sick.

If you loved me you would.

Do you want me to be happy?

We are all manipulators — but let me tell you why this realization matters.

Because relationships become healthier, less charged, less weighed down by tension and guilt when we ask for what we want without playing the game.

And mostly because attempting to control someone else is usually futile but always exhausting.

If you stop, everyone will do what they were going to do anyway and you will have energy left for other more hopeful endeavors.

Fighting for You

You are asking if you should break up with your boyfriend to see if he will fight for you.

If I break up with someone and he "fights for me" I keep the guy who overrides what I want, pushes on my personal boundaries and considers my decisions a suggestion.

If he doesn't fight for me, I have successfully eliminated a guy who respects my wishes.

Either way I needlessly hurt someone who cares for me.

I'm going to go with no.

What if You Have to Choose Between Your Partner or Your Writing?

This requires zero deliberation. My choice would take less than an instant.

My writing.

If someone truly loves me he wants what is best for me, rather than wanting to control me, possess me or dictate how I should spend my time.

I would choose my writing in a nanosecond not because my writing is more important than my partner but because rather than threatened and given ultimatums I should be supported and encouraged to do more of what I love.

Shifting Boundary

Imagine I'm dating a man who likes going out at night. I like him and going out with him is fun. He shows me many things I'm not normally exposed to — we go to new restaurants, dancing, the theater, stay up late.

As the novelty wears off, I begin to notice this is having an impact on my life. I can't get up early to write, I'm tired when I get to work, instead of going to yoga regularly I skip it to catch up on sleep.

This is taking a toll on my health.

One day I tell him that while I like him I need to adjust the dynamic he has become used to. I can go out sometimes, but not as frequently and not as late.

This is a new boundary. It's not consistent with the behavior I've shown him and yet it is just right.

His reaction will determine our compatibility.

If he respects my boundary he might say *"Yeah. Your health comes first and this adjustment sounds reasonable."* He might add *"I have been feeling overextended myself."*

If he does not respect my boundary, he might say *"I don't like this"* or even *"this has an impact over the relationship I imagined."*

I need to remain firm in my boundary. This is unrelated to how much I like him. If I say *"OK, let's just keep going out"* I am putting my health at risk. Given enough time, I will become someone different from the person he met.

Now, imagine if instead of saying *"I need to adjust this dynamic"* I say *"I need you to change. You cannot go out every night — it's not good for either of us."*

Instead of focusing the action on me, I want to adjust his way of life to suit my needs. Or, if you prefer, I want to adjust his way of life "for his own good".

Either way, that's not a boundary. That's attempting to exercise control on another person, and it is neither respectful nor healthy.

Secrets and Friends

My secrets belong to me. I decide if I want to share them or not and my decision is my boundary.

I might say *"I know you feel like me telling you my secrets will bring us closer together. You interpret me confiding in you as an act of intimacy. And, there are many things I am happy to tell you, but as the sole owner of my secrets I get to determine the pace, the time and the amount."*

Boundaries are difficult because they are not equal. For example, your friend might have no issue sharing everything with you — this is up to her and does not translate into an obligation for you to do the same.

Also, boundaries are hard because they are not static. How you feel about telling someone something might change, and that too is your right.

Open Relationship

After six years of marriage your spouse wants an open relationship and you don't and you are wondering what to do.

I am so very sorry for what you are going through. This sounds incredibly painful and maybe feels, aside from disconcerting and bewildering, also like a form of betrayal. It sounds different from the arrangement you originally agreed upon.

There are many lessons here.

The first is that everything changes, and people are no exception. People want one thing and then want another, and as we evolve we (often painfully) leave others behind.

There are no guarantees.

The second is that we cannot own another. No one belongs to us so it's not up to us to "allow", "give permission" or agree. People will do what they will do, with or without our consent.

The third is that being with someone who wants something different than what we want sets us up for regular, consistent, relentless pain and friction. Incompatibility is torture. It's not inflicted by the other person: we torture ourselves by staying.

I want to point out that this unfortunate development does not necessarily mean you are not loved. Someone can love you very much and still want to sleep with other people.

That it's important you spend some time to think about what you want for yourself and for your own life.

And that the worst part and the best part of all of this is that no one can tell you what to do but you.

It Bothers Me That My Friend Questions Me

If I have a friend who says or does anything that bothers me, the issue does not lie with my friend. It lies with me. Discomfort on my part is a sign that it's time for a boundary.

Here are some examples of what that might look like:

I understand you mean well but from now on please keep any concerns about how I live my life to yourself. If expressing your concerns continues, I will need some space.

I'm so excited to see you today! I don't want to talk about — .

You being in any way concerned about the decisions I make does not work for me.

If you disapprove of any of the choices that I make, I would appreciate you not bringing up your disapproval.

If you can't respect what I am asking for, I won't be spending time with you.

How Fair Is It to Love Someone Without Reciprocation?

Fair?

Any and all the unrequited love I feel — and any feeling I feel — is my responsibility.

If I love someone who doesn't feel the same way, what feels beautiful to me feels invasive to him.

What feels like an offering to me is an imposition to him.

What feels uplifting to me feels encroaching to him.

I don't want to take something buoyant and turn myself into a nuisance. I need to contain this, manage this, own this, or take myself somewhere else with this.

I cannot burden another with my brimming, spilling, sparking feelings. They are mine.

This doesn't mean I stop feeling them (mostly because I can't). But I do come to terms with the fact no one is obligated to reciprocate just because I feel them.

What if My Significant Other Can't Make Me a Priority?

If I meet a man and he has kids I sure hope his kids come first. I used to be that kid, and my father made sure his first consideration was me. His wife didn't need him like I needed him. Men who put their kids first are the kind of men I want.

If I meet a man and he has a passion, a deep interest that drives him, that makes him feel alive and filled with purpose, I sure hope his passion comes first. This means we will always have something new to talk about, that he will always have some interesting insight, but it also means we will love each other and support each other without being needy.

I need to be important to the people I am with but I am very comfortable not being their priority.

It used to matter a lot to me that I be the most important thing. But, you know what? I don't think there is any other notion quite as healthy or quite as liberating as the fact that I am not the center of the world.

Why Do I Attract People Who Put Pressure on Me?

I have a friend who adores being pursued. She relishes it from the get-go: the sense of being chosen, seeked out, knowing someone met her and considered her worthy of going after.

She likes the subsequent effort too. She doesn't always pick up the phone so the guy has to reach out more than once, she's not always available so the guy has to negotiate arrangements to see her, she acts coy, says no when she means yes, likes the feeling that someone is willing and interested enough to be persistent.

Then, once she's in the relationship, she feels the guy frequently puts pressure on her. *"He's insistent,"* she says, *"almost oppressive. Sometimes I feel badgered, harassed. He's pushy. He constantly forces past my boundaries."*

But, I say, that was your selection process.

I don't know anything about you and as such have no idea why you attract people who like to put pressure on you. What I can say is that we pick up twisted lessons about love and relationships — play hard to get! — and then end up with what we have inadvertently chosen.

His Teasing Isn't Funny Anymore.
What Do I Do?

There was this guy I really liked and whenever he asked if we could hang out I'd say yes. Yes!

To hang out with him I moved everything else. I was planning on doing some work at that time but I will reorganize myself. I was planning on going somewhere else but I can do that tomorrow.

I'd just say yes.

After some time, I began to feel resentful. I am overextending myself to accommodate this person. And I want to see him, but I wish it would cost me less. I wish I didn't have to sacrifice other things in order to see him.

But, you know what? He had no way of knowing that sometimes seeing him meant I was canceling something.

I was not setting boundaries. I was just saying yes.

Without boundaries, and with my excessive enthusiasm, I am laying the groundwork for this relationship to make me bitter and resentful and exhausted.

All unbeknownst to him.

I don't know anything about your situation and don't want to make any assumptions. But your question states "it's not even

257

funny anymore." Was it once funny? Did you lead him to believe that you at one point found his teasing funny?

Because, he might simply not know he is hurting you, and is instead trying to make you laugh.

Again, I have no context so only you have the measure of what is taking place.

Being teased is very painful and I don't intend to make less of that. It's just that I find it helpful to look at what I've been doing and how I might do it differently before I conclude that another person is deliberately hurting me.

Often, the person who set things up that way is me.

Control

If someone wants to control me, they want to exercise authority or domination over me or something that's mine. They want to keep me in check and reduce my ability to flourish.

Control comes from insecurity. *If I can limit you, I can keep you. If I can dominate you, I won't lose you.*

Except, control doesn't work. It takes the oxygen out of a relationship, suffocating it.

The moment you believe something belongs to you or that you need to control it, you will eventually lose it.

If you want to know if someone is trying to control you — or if what you are doing is trying to control someone else — here are some questions to ask yourself.

Do you feel heard, respected, considered? Is there snooping or spying? Are you frequently accused, or criticized, *"for your own good"*? Is discomfort handled through threats? (*If you do that, I will leave you.*)

Is your relationship affecting the dynamic of other relationships, like you see your friends less because your significant other doesn't like them?

Does your significant other interpret you needing alone time as you not prioritizing the relationship?

Are your efforts to take care of yourself sabotaged?

Do you feel like someone in the relationship is constantly keeping score? Is love made conditional? Are guilt trips common?

Exercising control is very different from setting boundaries. Boundaries outline my limits. Control is an attempt to outline yours.

Is It Weird if Your Partner Tells You Exactly What to Do?

It's not weird. It's extremely common. It's also controlling, possessive, and possibly unsafe.

If someone cares about your well-being in a way that is healthy, here is what it looks like:

There is a sense of sovereignty.

You feel free, seen, heard, respected, trusted.

Clear boundaries have been established and observed by both parties. Disagreeing or saying no is not a cause for stress or tension.

Space is both requested and granted without friction, guilt, angst, shame or fear.

We feel responsible for our behavior and do not "own" the behavior of the other.

There is room for each person to have very different opinions and beliefs.

Each person gets to grow and evolve in the way they think is best with the support and company — not the direction — of the other person.

Is Disrespecting Someone Who Disrespects You a Boundary?

Creating a boundary is anything that clearly outlines your limits. It's typically designed for you to be able to give the best of yourself. Here are some examples:

I really want to stay longer but I'm going to call it a night as I have to get up early tomorrow.

We've been arguing for a while and I'm getting burned out. This conversation is really important to me but I'm going to need a break from it.

Mom, I love you very much but I don't want to talk to you about my relationship.

Now, toxic behavior is defined as anything that is likely to make things worse, to be hurtful, to focus on retaliation instead of a resolution. Disrespecting someone who disrespects you is not a boundary — it's an example of toxic behavior.

Is "No" a Complete Sentence?

Imagine if you will that a guy and I are kissing. Not with affection. With passion. This is not a peck on the cheek. This is smooching. This is necking. This is full on making out.

Rawr.

I feel his hand slide up my back, glide down my shoulder and land squarely on my breast. My boob. My melon. My knocker.

I push his hand away and say *"no"*.

At this point you might wonder if I have a good reason to say no. Do I have a headache? Am I not in the mood?

Is this fair? Is this right? Is nothing sacred anymore?

What is happening?

My answer is that it doesn't matter. This requires no explanation. None. This rack, this objectively luscious scoop of flesh belongs to me.

I have complete and total independence, absolute, uncontested sovereignty and power over every inch of me.

And this is why my answer to your question is yes.

"No" is a complete sentence.

How Would You Distinguish Aggressive From Assertive?

Aggressive tends towards attack. It's threatening. It's competitive. It's full of judgment and spills emotion. It's combative, invasive, contentious. It's really insecure.

Shut up. You have to see things my way.

Assertive is clear and strong, positive and self-assured. It stands its ground but does not need to provoke. It's self-aware. I don't need to railroad you or shut you down. Your opinion doesn't make less of mine.

How Can You Tell if You're Developing Self-Awareness?

Symptoms of increased self-awareness:

I am clearer on how things make me feel. What makes me feel good? What makes me feel anxious? How does being around that person make me feel? How does doing this (nurtured, happy, healthy) or that (guilty, nervous) make me feel?

I used to feel and instantly react. *Now, wait a minute. I feel anger. Why? Where is this coming from? Is the thought or series of thoughts that caused this anger real? Is this something I can breathe through? How can I best represent myself?*

I am getting better at recognizing the voice of my ego. *Oh my god I am alone. What are people going to think of me? Why doesn't anyone understand me?* It's OK, ego. You are not alone. You never will be. I've got you.

I used to feel despair when someone misunderstood me or expressed disappointment. Now, I can watch that sensation. Can I make room in this tight, cavernous space? Can it be OK, to be misunderstood? Can I stand by the boundary I just created for myself?

Speaking of which, I am getting better at creating boundaries, at saying no to things so I have more space for myself — even when it feels scary or makes me feel like I'm being selfish.

I begin to do things I am scared of.

I have plans for myself and am following through on them.

I'm sad and very tired when I think of all the things I used to do that I couldn't see. My past behavior, my past suffering, my patterns.

Spending time alone used to make me feel restless and trapped. Now I love it, need it, crave it. Spending time alone feels wonderful but even when it doesn't I know it's solace: a steady place to go to sort myself out.

What Does Healing Mean to You and When Can You Finally Say You've Healed?

I don't think any emotional process is linear or has a clear beginning or end. It's more of a dance, a one step two step towards progress, two or three steps back, being gentle with myself and realizing — well. I need to begin again.

Here are a few things I do that indicate to me I am on the right track:

I am grateful instead of bitter or resentful. This can even be a flash of gratitude in an ocean of anger. That flash is the point to walk towards.

When I say "no". The more comfortable I am with whatever boundary I am setting, the better the place I am in. Another way to put this is that I begin to be at peace with being misunderstood or with disappointing someone in the name of standing up for myself.

When I can see my feeling or my thought approach and I distinguish it from me. *Oh, look. I feel sad today.* This sadness is transitory. I feel sad is different from I am sad.

When I am able to see someone else react in a way that would typically be hurtful and can dismiss it because I can tell it's not related to me. My co-worker is frustrated, and that doesn't mean he's frustrated at me.

I like being alone. I'm not restless, pacing, desperate for distractions. I'm enjoying my own company.

All this is happening and I am humming along and feeling quite peaceful and proud of myself and then I do something or say something and I think *"I did it again."*

So, I start over.

You can always start over.

About the Author

Dushka Zapata has worked in communications for over twenty years, running agencies (such as Edelman and Ogilvy) and working with companies to develop their corporate strategy.

During this time she specialized in executive equity and media and presentation training. She helped people communicate better through key message refinement and consistency and coached them to smoothly manage difficult interviews with press during times of crisis.

Dushka is an executive coach and public speaker who imparts workshops about personal brand development. She has been hired for strategic alignment hiring, to coach and mentor high potential individuals, improve upon new business pitches, refine existing processes and galvanize a company's communication efforts.

She recently built and ran the communications team at Zendesk and is now head of communications for Forte, a start up that believes games can unlock new economic opportunities for billions of people.

Dushka is the author of ten books: "How to be Ferociously Happy", "Amateur: an inexpert, inexperienced, unauthoritative, enamored view of life", "A Spectacular Catastrophe and other things I recommend", "Your Seat Cushion is a Flotation Device and other buoyant short stories", "Someone Destroyed My Rocket Ship and other havoc I have witnessed at the office", "How to Build a Pillow Fort and other valuable life lessons", "You Belong Everywhere and other things you'll have to see for yourself", "Love Yourself and other insurgent acts that recast everything", "Feelings Are Fickle and other things I wish someone had told me", and the one you have in your hands.

Dushka was recently named one of the top 25 innovators in her industry by The Holmes Report and regularly contributes to Quora, the question and answer site, where she has over 169 million views.

Printed in Great Britain
by Amazon

79024050R00164